Islam & Christianity:
Conflict or Conciliation?

Islam & Christianity: Conflict or Conciliation?

A Comparative and Textual Analysis of the Koran & the Bible

Muhammed A. Asadi

Writers Club Press
San Jose New York Lincoln Shanghai

Islam & Christianity: Conflict or Conciliation?
A Comparative and Textual Analysis of the Koran & the Bible

All Rights Reserved © 2001 by Muhammed A. Asadi

No part of this book may be reproduced or transmitted in any form or by any means, graphic, electronic, or mechanical, including photocopying, recording, taping, or by any information storage retrieval system, without the permission in writing from the publisher.

Writers Club Press
an imprint of iUniverse, Inc.

For information address:
iUniverse, Inc.
5220 S. 16th St., Suite 200
Lincoln, NE 68512
www.iuniverse.com

ISBN: 0-595-21258-1

Printed in the United States of America

*The Koran, the source of Islam, from the beginning has sought conciliation with the "People of the Book." It presented itself as "all-inclusive" to members of all religions based on their sincerity in accepting the truth when it gets to them. In this context, it states that all those who believe in God and the last day, regardless of label, will have nothing to fear. Christians are termed as the "closest" to the Muslims in "love"(compared to all other groups). Mary, the mother of Jesus is honored in the Koran as, "**a woman chosen above the women of all nations**" (Koran 3:42). Such honor for Mary is not to be found in the Holy Bible itself. The Koran terms Jesus as one of the greatest of God's messengers and celebrates his birth and mission, terming him an exemplary human being (Koran 19:53).*

Contents

Preface ix

CHAPTER 1   HISTORICAL/TEXTUAL ANALYSIS OF THE BIBLE: 1
IS IT GOD'S WORD?

CHAPTER 2   JESUS IN THE KORAN & THE BIBLE: . 31
IS JESUS GOD?

CHAPTER 3   PAUL AND THE INVENTION OF CHRISTIANITY 51

CHAPTER 4   WOMEN & RELIGION: 61
KORAN & THE OPPRESSED WOMAN

CHAPTER 5   MEDIA TERRORISM: 87
WHAT IS JIHAD?

CHAPTER 6   SCIENTIFIC REVELATION: 93
KORAN & CRITICAL RATIONALISM

Preface

Growing up in Pakistan, due to the diffusion of Western culture, the legacy of Colonialism, I became well aware of the "traditional" Western claims against Islam. To many Muslims in the "Third World", these claims have resulted in an inferiority complex. As a result, they must emulate the West and the religion of the West, in order to cure their "disease". Christian missionaries are well aware of this and usually take advantage of it. They may criticize the ways of the so-called "free society" while at home in the West, but in Muslim lands they present these "freedoms" as a consequence of Christianity.

Muslims are generally unaware of the historical conflict between freedom, science and Christianity. Ironically, they are also unaware that the history of modern science began with the Koran. Muslims inspired by the Koran did pioneering foundation building work in all fields of modern science, thus sparking the European Renaissance. The majority of Muslims live within countries whose regimes are as oppressive as they are against Islam, and as such, they fall easy prey to Christian propaganda, at times disguised as "human-relief" or charity. The German philosopher, Fredrick Nietzsche was well aware of the harms Christianity's relationship to learning and freedom:

> *Not only did Christianity deprive us of the benefits of Roman culture, says Nietzsche, but of those of Islam as well. The rich Moorish culture in Spain was trampled down "because it said Yes to life." It was a culture from which Christendom could and should have learned much. The crusades were fought against a culture that "the crusaders would have done better to lie down in the dust before." An unstated real motivation behind the Crusades was to plunder the wealth of the Near East; Nietzsche refers to the Cru-*

sades as *"higher piracy." [A 60, **http://www.debunker.com/ texts/anti_chr.html**, retreived 12/08/'01]*

The source of the conflict between Islam and Christianity are the historical stereotypes about Islam, usually quick and cheap excuses to lure people into Christianity. The culprits here are not the masses in the Christian world but the Christian missionaries. Evangelical Christian missionaries do not represent Jesus, according to my readings of his words and my experience with them. Similarly, Muslim preachers in mosques in "Third World" countries do not represent the words of the Koran.

The Koran from the beginning has sought conciliation with the "People of the Book." It presented itself as "all-inclusive" to members of all faiths based on their sincerity in accepting the truth when it gets to them. In this context, it states that all those who believe in God and the last day, regardless of label, will have nothing to fear. Christians are termed as the "closest" to the Muslims in "love" (compared to all other groups). Mary, the mother of Jesus is honored in the Koran as, *"a woman chosen above the women of all nations."* Such honor for Mary is not to be found in the Holy Bible itself. The Koran terms Jesus as one of the greatest of God's messengers and celebrates his birth and mission.

The major difference between Islam and Christianity revolves around the nature of Jesus. The Koran terms Jesus as a messenger of God, a mortal. It does not accept the Christian claim that God (immortal) becomes man (mortal), or that God begets offspring. The Koran presents reasons and encourages rational inquiry. This book is an attempt to state those reasons and to dispel common stereotypes held against Islam, which have no basis in reality.

This work is also an attempt at conciliation with those who study the historical Jesus, members of the Jesus Seminar for example. A textual analysis of the source books of Islam and Christianity shows that we have more in common, if we follow the sayings and doings of the historical Jesus, than is realized. The Koran is the bridge over which traditional Christians and scholars of the historical Jesus can approach each other's territory, safely and in harmony with the core sayings of Jesus.

Muhammed Asadi
Copyright © 2001

1

HISTORICAL/TEXTUAL ANALYSIS OF THE BIBLE:

IS IT GOD'S WORD?

In his book, *Is the Bible God's Word?* Dr. William Scroggie of the Moody Bible Institute in Chicago, states:

> *Yes, the Bible is human, though some out of zeal, which is not according to knowledge, have rejected this. Those books have passed through the minds of men, are written in the language of men, were penned by the hands of men, and bear in their style, the characteristics of men. (Page 17)*

The Bible comes in many versions. Some common ones are the King James Version, the Revised Standard Version, the New International Version, the American Standard, the Catholic (Douay) and the Good News Bible etc. If the Bible is indeed the word of God, then we need to ask, "which version is from God?" The different versions of the Bible are not merely different translations. They add and take out what other "versions" contain.

The most common among the Bibles in the world is the King James Version and its many major revisions. It was first published in 1611. It is the only Bible that has been translated in over fifteen hundred different languages of the world. The King James Version (KJV) has 66 books bound together within its covers. Compare this to the Roman

Catholic Version (Douay) of the Bible which has 73 books bound within its covers. Seven whole books have been removed from the King James (a Protestant version of the Bible) that the Douay Version includes. Protestants have expunged these books from their Bible, calling them "Apocrypha" or "weak" in authority.

The Bible within its text never claims to be one uniform book. Nowhere within the text of the Bible is the Bible called "The Bible". The word Bible itself was invented to represent a collection of books. As we saw above, this collection of books was not the same among different groups. Compare this to the Koran; there is not a word of difference between two Koran's anywhere in the world. The Koran is the only thing common among Muslims of whatever nationality, sect or group. The Koran within its text names itself over fifty times as "The Koran". It also claims to be completely from God, as a whole (Koran 55:2 etc.).

> *"In any event, none of [the original manuscripts of the books of the Bible] now survive. What do survive are copies made over the course of centuries, or more accurately, <u>copies of the copies of the copies</u>, some 5,366 of them in the Greek language alone, that date from the second century down to the sixteenth. Strikingly, with the exception of the smallest fragments, <u>no two of these copies are exactly alike in their particulars</u>. No one knows how many differences, or variant readings, occur among the surviving witnesses, but they must number in the hundreds of thousands."*
> ——[The Orthodox Corruption of Scripture, Bart Ehrman, pp. 27, from **http://www.plaintruth.org**, 12/07/01]

There are about 24000 manuscripts of the New Testament in the Greek that are termed "original". However the fact is that these "originals" are themselves copies of documents that have now been lost. Also, no two of these 24000 "originals" are identical. They are not even self-consistent. To substantiate this claim, one need not be a scholar of the history of the Bible. Any modern version of the New Testament has footnotes that clearly state after most statements, "*Other ancient manuscripts add...*" or "*Other ancient manuscripts delete...*" or "*Other ancient manuscripts insert...*" Which manuscript out of these is from God and who did the additions and deletions?

The Koran in its history and transmission is very different to the Bible:

1. The Koran is present in a living language, Arabic. Over 250 million people speak the language of the Koran. Hundreds of millions more study the classical script of the book, making the Koran the "most read" book on earth (ironically the least understood).

2. The Koran has always been in the possession of the people, the masses and not only the elite, as there is no priesthood in Islam. The Bible on the other hand has always been the possession of the Church elite, where it got shaped, modified and passed on based on Church authority.

   "...Not so the New Testament...There is condensation and editing; there is choice in reproduction and witness. The Gospels have come through the mind of the Church behind the authors. They represent experience and history..."
   —[The Call of the Minaret, Kenneth Cragg, p 277, from http://www.plaintruth.org, 12/06/'01]

3. There is not a word of difference between two Arabic Koran's anywhere in the world. The Koran is the only unifying force among Muslims. Muslims frequently disagree on everything else except the Arabic wording of the Koran. However, in the case of the Bible, ancient manuscripts are not identical, no two "copies" of the so-called originals are the same. Footnotes in all modern versions of the Bible clearly document the differences.

The "Most Ancient" Manuscripts:

The Revised Standard Version (RSV) of the Bible first appeared in 1952. The editors claimed in the preface that it went to the "most ancient manuscripts" of the Bible. By "most ancient" they mean those that date 200 to 300 years after Jesus. "Ancient" manuscripts on the other hand, on which the King James Version was based, date 400 to 600 years after Jesus. All scholars agree that none of the originals of any of the manuscripts exist. All we have are "most ancient" and "ancient" copies.

The preface to the RSV says that it was produced by thirty two scholars of "the highest eminence", backed by "fifty cooperating denominations (of Christianity)." Historically, since the RSV goes back to the "most ancient" manuscripts it is more accurate than the KJV. About halfway down the preface of the RSV, on page one, these fifty-two scholars unanimously declare:

> *The King James Version has grave defects…and that these defects are so many and so serious as to call for a revision (1952:1)*

The Grave Defects:

If we look at the New Testament section of the RSV, we see that the only "proof" from the Bible that the Christian fundamentalists had of the concept of the Trinity has been removed. The "most-ancient" manuscripts never had this passage (1st Epistle of John 5:7). However, as Christianity got Romanized and moved away from pure monotheism, the elite who possessed authority on what becomes doctrine shoved this statement in:

> *"For there are three that bear record in heaven, the Father, the Son and the Holy Ghost, and these three are one." (New Testament, 1John 5:7)*

Not only the RSV but also all modern versions of the Bible do not contain this statement anymore. It has been unceremoniously thrown out. By doing this the scholars are not only bringing Christianity closer to Islam, they are confirming the part of the Koran that says:

"And do not say Trinity, desist from this, it will be better for you, for God is one God (Waahid in Arabic)." (Koran 4:171)

Another thing that we notice in the RSV, that goes to the "most-ancient" manuscripts is that the word "begotten" in the famous verse in John (3:16) has been taken out. John 3:16, in the King James Version (KJV) reads:

"For God so loved the world that he gave his only <u>begotten</u> son..."(New Testament, John 3:16)

By removing the word "begotten" from this verse, the scholars of Christianity are once again coming closer to Islam. The Koran states that God doesn't adopt or beget sons or daughters. The concept of "son" and an uncreated, eternal "God" are mutually exclusive, logically speaking. God represents one who received life from no one, while son signifies one who got existence from another source. In the literal sense of the word, no one can claim to be God and son at the same time.

In the language of the Jews however, the word "son" has a metaphoric meaning as well. Thus, the term "son of God" is used in the Bible, both Old and New Testaments to signify good, righteous people. Jesus himself is quoted as saying, "Blessed are the peace-makers for they shall be called sons of God." (Matthew 5:9). The word that was causing difference in John 3:16 was the word "begotten". The scholars "of the highest eminence" are informing us that this was an interpolation, a later addition to the text of the statement.

In the 1952 version of the RSV, the first eleven verses of the 8th chapter of the Gospel of John have been removed. The chapter now begins at verse 12. The scholars explained that these eleven verses were interpolations, later additions to the manuscript of John. As a result they are now in the footnote and not the text of the 1952 RSV. Also taken out are the only two references in the gospels to the ascension of Jesus (Mark 16:19 and Luke 24:51). They are taken out as interpolations as well.

In 1971 they revised the RSV, and this time due to pressure from certain denominations, they added back the eleven verses of the 8th chapter of John that were taken out. This "game" of adding and taking out has been going on for centuries. The construction of "God's word" has also been a prosperous industry. It is precisely for this reason that the Koran warns us:

> *Woe unto those who write the book with their own hands and then say, "This is from God," that they may trade it for some miserable gain. Woe to them for what their hands do write and woe to them for what they earn with it." (Koran 2:79)*

According to the doctrine of most Christian denominations, the first five books of the Bible, i.e. Genesis, Exodus, Leviticus, Numbers and Deuteronomy were "written" by Moses and are called the "Books of Moses". However, scholars don't attribute any of these books to Moses at all. Internal evidence in these books makes it clear that Moses could not have written these words. In the 34th chapter of the Book of Deuteronomy, we read:

> *"So Moses the servant of the lord **died**...and He (i.e. God) buried Him...and there arose not a prophet since in Israel like unto Moses." (Deuteronomy 34:5-10)*

Moses could not have written these words (his obituary), written in the past tense, after he had died! Also the word "since" in the verse clearly shows that whoever is writing this lived long after Moses had died. All through these five books, the structure of the sentences as well as the "third-person" reference to Moses and to God shows that neither

God nor Moses wrote these words. Sentences, repeated hundreds of times, "God said unto Moses and Moses said unto the Lord," in these five books, clearly shows that a third person, someone other than God and Moses is writing these words.

Also, consider these words in the Book of Numbers, thought to have been written by Moses:

> *Now the man Moses was very meek, above all the men which were upon the face of the earth." (Numbers 12:3)*

The meekest man on the face of the earth would never say that he was meek. Moreover, the meek man does not appear to be very meek in the judgments that he gives in the same book of the Bible:

> *"And Moses was wroth…And Moses said unto them, "Have ye saved all the women alive? … Now therefore kill every male among the little ones, and kill every woman, … But all the female children … keep alive for yourselves." Numbers 31: 14-18*

What about the Gospels?

J. B Phillip, a prebendary of the Chichester cathedral in England, a paid servant of the Anglican Church, in his, *New Testament in Modern English (1996)*, states in the preface to the gospel according to Matthew:

> *"Early tradition ascribed this gospel to the apostle Matthew, but scholars nowadays almost all reject this view…The author, whom we can <u>conveniently</u> call Matthew has plainly drawn on the mysterious "Q", which may have been a collection of oral traditions. He has used Mark's gospel freely"*

J.B Phillip is telling us clearly that Matthew didn't write Matthew. We don't know the source or the author of this anonymous book. He is further stating that whoever has written this gospel (one that can be conveniently called Matthew), has plagiarized Mark.

Not only do modern scholars reject that idea that Matthew wrote Matthew, internal evidence in this gospel clearly shows that someone other than Matthew (and other than Jesus) wrote it. Consider the 9th verse of the 9th chapter of Matthew:

> *"And as Jesus passed forth thence, He (i.e. Jesus) saw a man called Matthew sitting at the receipt of custom, and he (Jesus) said to him (Matthew), "Follow me," and he (Matthew) arose and followed him (i.e. Jesus)." (New Testament, Matthew 9:9)*

The "Third-Person" reference to Jesus and Matthew, the hes and the hims, clearly shows that whoever is writing this is not Jesus and is not Matthew. The same situation is encountered while reading the gospel of John, in at least two places:

> i) *"And <u>he</u> that saw it bare record, and <u>his</u> record is true, and <u>he</u> knows that <u>he</u> says the truth so that you may believe (John 19:35)*

> ii) *"This is the disciple who testifies of these things, and who wrote these things, and **we** know that <u>his</u> testimony is true." (John 21:24-25)*

The "third person" reference to the witness of events shows that the writer is either copying or editing the narration of "he that saw it." Who are these "we"?

The author of the gospel of Luke does not claim inspiration of his gospel writing from God. He says that he wrote it because he knew of the events and it "seemed good to him" (Luke 1:1-5). Also see 1 Corinthians 7:25 where Paul, in this specific case says that he's informing without God's commandment. 2 Timothy 3:16 is presented to "prove" that the entire Bible is God's inspiration, the above 2 references apart from the many others disprove that.

> "Many scholars think the gospels are unreliable records since they were written as proclamation, not objective history, decades after Jesus' death." (In search of Jesus, U.S.News & World Report, April 8 1996, page 47)

> "There are, after all, four Gospels, whose actual writing, most scholars have come to acknowledge, was done not by the Apostles but by their anonymous followers (or their follower's followers). Each presented a somewhat different picture of Jesus' life. (The search for Jesus, TIME, April 8 1996, page 38)

Language of the New Testament:

Jesus spoke Aramaic; therefore the general implication that arises is that his gospel would be in Aramaic, which is very close to Arabic, the language of the Koran. However, all the manuscripts of the present-day New Testament are in Koine Greek. If Jesus spoke Aramaic, why are his gospels in Greek? Why are there gospels in the plural when Jesus spoke of one gospel (Mark 10:29etc.)? Which gospel is the "word of God" since they add or take away from each other and even contradict each other?

There are certain chapters in the Bible that are attributed to different authors, in different periods of history, yet they are 100% identical. This shows that "editors" were at work in manufacturing what would later become the word of God. For example, 2 Kings 19 and Isaiah 37 are identical word by word, sentence by sentence, throughout the whole chapter.

However, even though there is not even a sentence that is identical between the Koran and the Bible, and there were no Arabic Bibles available in Muhammed's day, the Christian missionaries accuse Muhammed of copying the Bible. Alas, he left out all the contradictions, the pornography and the scientific errors. He also left out the "double standards" in the Old Testament morality regarding Jews and gentiles[1]. There are many direct parallels between the New Testament and the Old, yet no missionary accuses the gospel writers of "borrowing" even though they did even from each other. The fact is that the Koran and the Bible are not the same, they are very different. The accusation that Muhammed copied the Bible is baseless.

Contradictions:

According to the assumptions about God in the Bible itself, i.e. God being all knowing, and not the "author of confusion", any book that claims to be from God should be free from mistakes and contradictions. However, the Bible is full of scientific and logical errors and contradictions among and within its various books. Here are a few examples:

Old Testament:

1. God or Satan?
   2 Samuel 24:1 in the Old Testament of the Bible says that God incited David to take a census of the Jews, i.e. to number Israel. 1Chronicles 21:1 however, says that "Satan" inspired David to conduct the census. God and Satan are not synonyms in any religion.

2. Was Jehoiachin 8 or 18?
   2 Chronicles 36:9 in the Old Testament says that a guy named Jehoiachin was 8 years old when he became king. However, 2 Kings 24:8 in the same Old Testament says that he was 18 when he became king.

3. Was it Cavalry or Infantry? Was it 700 or 7000?
   2 Samuel 10:18 states that David slew the men of 700 chariots of

---

1. The Old Testament and Judaism are well known for their racist attitude towards all non-Jews. One example is the passage in the Torah ,which states that interest on money lent cannot be charged from Jews but can be charged from Gentiles (The Bible, Deuteronomy 23:19-21).

the Syrians and 40,000 horsemen (cavalry) including Shobach the commander. However 2 Chronicles 19:18 of the same Old Testament of the Bible states that he slew the men of 7000 chariots and 40,000 footmen (infantry) and the commander Shobach. How many were they and was it infantry or cavalry? Who made the mistake, an all knowing God or humanity?

4. How many stalls for horses did Solomon have? Was it 4000 or 40,000?
1 Chronicles 9:25 in the Bible says that Solomon had 4000 stalls for horses and chariots. 1 Kings 4:26 however, states that he had 40,000 stalls for horses.

5. Did Arah have 775 sons or 652?
Ezra 2:5 of the Bible states that Arah, an exile, had 775. However Nehemiah 7:10 states that he had 652. The lists are the same, yet the numbers are different. Who made the mistake? Was it God?

6. Were humans created before or after the animals?
Man was created AFTER the other animals (Genesis 1:25-26)
Man was created BEFORE the other animals (Genesis 2:18-19).

New Testament:

1. John the Baptist contradicts Jesus!
According to Jesus, John the Baptist was Elijah in the Second Coming (Matthew 17:11). John the Baptist however, denied being Elijah when the Priests and the Levites questioned him (John 1:19-21). Here Jesus contradicts John the Baptist. Who was lying? Jesus, John or the author who lived much after the events?

2. Cross or Tree?
Was Jesus put on a cross, *Stauron* in Greek (Mark 15:21) or was he put on a tree, *Ksulon* in Greek (1 Peter 2:24).

3. Ascension, none or some?
   John 3:13 quotes Jesus as saying the no one ascended into heaven except the son of man (himself) who descended from heaven. This contradicts 2 Kings 2:11 of the Old Testament of the Bible, which says that Elijah, ascended into heaven.

4. What were Jesus' last words?
   Matthew 27:46,50: "And about the ninth hour Jesus cried with a loud voice, saying, "Eli, Eli, lama sabachthani?" that is to say, "My God, my God, why hast thou forsaken me?" ...Jesus, when he cried again with a loud voice, yielded up the ghost."

   Luke 23:46: "And when Jesus had cried with a loud voice, he said, "Father, unto thy hands I commend my spirit:" and having said thus, he gave up the ghost."

   John 19:30: "When Jesus therefore had received the vinegar, he said, "It is finished:" and he bowed his head, and gave up the ghost."

   Were the last words, "My God, my God.." or were they "Father into thy hands.." or were they "It is finished" ?

5. The Genealogy of Jesus: 41 ancestors or 26?
   Luke in describing the genealogy of Jesus gives 41 names (ancestors) being the forefathers of Jesus. However, Matthew describing the genealogy of the same Jesus gives only 26 names. A difference of 15 ancestors.
   Luke in his gospel claims that from Abraham to Jesus there were 14+14+14, i.e. 42 ancestors, yet if you count the names that he gives, he mentions only 41 and forgot the 42nd! Both Luke and Matthew trace this genealogy through the same man, Joseph the carpenter who according to both Islam and Christianity had no part to play in the birth of Jesus. The gospels clearly state that Joseph the carpenter was not Jesus' father, why trace a genealogy

that is incorrect from the very beginning? In these two lists, except for the name of Joseph, no two names are identical. They are separate lists, yet they claim to trace the genealogy of the same man. Matthew mentions that Jesus was the "seed" of David through Solomon, while Luke says that he was the "seed" of David through Nathan (Solomon's brother). The "seed" of David however, could never reach Jesus through Solomon and Nathan (his brother) at the same time. According to Matthew, Jesus' grandfather is Jacob (who was the father of Joseph the carpenter), while according to Luke it is Heli who is the grandfather of Jesus. There are numerous such contradictions in the two genealogies alone.

6. Can God be seen or not?
   "No man hath seen God at any time." (John 1:18)

   "And he said, Thou canst not see my face; for there shall no man see me and live." (Ex. 33:20)

   "Whom no man hath seen nor can see." (1 Tim. 6:16)

   Compare the above to:

   "And I will take away my hand, and thou shalt see my backparts." (Exodus. 33:23)

   "And the Lord spake to Moses face to face, as a man speaketh to his friend." (Exodus 3:11)

   "For I have seen God face to face, and my life is preserved." (Genesis 32:30)

7. To judge or not to judge:
   1 Corinthians 3:15 " The spiritual man makes judgments about all things, but he himself is not subject to any man's judgment:"

1 Corinthians 4:5 " Therefore judge nothing before the appointed time; wait till the Lord comes. He will bring to light what is hidden in darkness and will expose the motives of men's hearts. At that time each will receive his praise from God."

8. The Second Coming of Jesus:
   Verily I say unto you, This generation shall not pass, till all these things are fulfilled. Matthew 24:34

   Verily I say unto you, that this generation shall not pass, till all these things be done. Mark 13:30

   Verily I say unto you, This generation shall not pass away, till all be fulfilled.
   Luke 21:32

   How many generations have passed since those words were written, yet there has been no Second Coming yet!
   "For another, the post-resurrection stories contain a variety of factual discrepancies about the main characters, places, times and the messages attributed to the Risen Jesus. For example, the Gospel of Matthew has Jesus appearing first to Mary Magdalene and other woman. Luke gives the first appearance to Peter, and (with the exception of a later addition to his Gospel) Mark contains no post-Resurrection appearances at all. Luke's Gospel says that Jesus appeared to the apostles in the Jerusalem area; Matthew says it was in Galilee." (Rethinking the Resurrection, Newsweek. April 8 1996, page 44)

9. Did Jesus deliver the sermon:
   On the MOUNT (Matthew 5:1-2) or on a PLAIN (Luke 6:17-20).

10. Was the woman Greek or not?
    Was it a GREEK woman who sought Jesus since her daughter was ill (Mark 7:26) or was it a woman of CANAAN (Mark 15:22).

Some Scientific Errors in the Bible:

If the Bible had a human origin, as this chapter claims, then we should be able to find numerous scientific errors in its text, given its history. Bertrand Russell, in his book, *Why I am not a Christian*, noticed that the Bible mentioned that the hare chewed cud, when it reality it didn't:

> *Yet of those that <u>chew the cud</u> or have the hoof cloven you shall not eat these: the camel, <u>the hare</u>, and the rock badger, <u>because they chew the cud</u> but do not part the hoof, are unclean for you" (Deuteronomy 14:7)*

If we look at the creation account given in Genesis we find numerous scientific errors. Genesis is not a coherent whole. The first five books of the Bible, scholars say, are a combination of different sources, authored at different periods in time, yet are combined and mixed as books:

> *In 1854, four sources were recognized (for the first five books of the Bible). They were called the Yahvist version (9th century BC), the Elohist version (little earlier than the Yahvist), Deuteronomy (8th century BC), and the Sacerdotal version (around the Sixth century BC). (as stated in Bucaille, 1982)*

Old Testament scholars recognize that there are two different versions on creation given in the Book of Genesis. The *Yahwist* narration is the older of the two, the other one being the *Sacerdotal* narration. Scholars have concluded that the *Sacerdotal* version was the work of priests, the spiritual successors of the prophet Ezekiel.

The *Sacerdotal* version contains genealogies that go back to Adam that are scientifically unacceptable because they set a figure for the age of the world (5738 years) and when man appeared on earth, that are proven to be false. The appearance of man can be measured in tens of thousands of years, while the earth is at least 4.5 billion years old.

The Biblical narration about the creation of the universe (Genesis 1) also contradicts what has been established by modern science. The Bible mentions "primordial waters", something cosmologists do not accept (Genesis 1:1-2). It mentions "light" being created on the first day, before the creation of the stars which are responsible for the light in the universe. Light is mentioned on the first day, while stars do not get formed until day four (Genesis 1:14-19). Its mention of the existence of an evening and a morning before the creation of the Sun, is inaccurate. It mentions the creation of the earth on the "third" day and the sun on the "fourth" (Genesis 1:14-19), which is incorrect scientifically as well. The Earth and the Moon had their origin in the Sun.

The mention of plants, "yielding seed according to their own kinds," on the third day (Genesis 1: 9-13), i.e. before the creation of the Sun on the fourth is also inaccurate scientifically speaking. Plants cannot exist without the Sun. Also, the appearance of birds together with sea creatures, before the land animals, is inaccurate (Genesis 1: 20-31).

Contrary to the Bible, the Koran gives an accurate description of the creation of the universe from one unit, the expanding universe and pre-empts much of today's hard-earned scientific facts in cosmology (for details see **http://www.rationalreality.com**, and Chapter 5).

Paleontologists have established that mammals came first and then birds, yet the Bible states that the birds came on the "fifth" day and the beasts of the earth came on the "sixth". These are the results of beliefs prevalent at the time and have nothing to do with being the words of an all-knowing creator.

About Noah, the Bible speaks of a universal flood that occurred roughly 300 years before Abraham. This would correspond to the 21st or the 22nd century BC. In view of all the historical data that we have, the universal flood never happened. How can we believe that in the

21st and 22nd century BC, all of civilization was destroyed when the history of the Egyptians is unbroken all through this time.

> *In the case of Egypt for example, the remains correspond to the period preceding the Middle Kingdom (2,100 BC) at roughly the date of the First Intermediate Period before the Eleventh Dynasty. In Babylonia it is the Third Dynasty at Ur. We know for certain that there was no break in these civilizations, so that there could have been no destruction affecting the whole of humanity, as it appears in the Bible (Bucaille, 1982).*

Contrary to the Biblical description, the Koran mentions that only the people of Noah were destroyed by the flood and not all of humanity. We have historical evidence of such floods in that general area but no universal floods.

Contrary to the Bible, the description of the natural world in the Koran is amazingly accurate and pre-empts much of today's hard-earned scientific findings. Consistent with Karl Popper's *Critical Rationalism*, the Koran offers falsification. As such, it challenges people of learning to find fault with it and to falsify it. This point will be addressed in chapter 5.

The Bible & Terror:

These and many other passages in the Bible would get an "X" rating for violence and pornography from even the most lenient and liberal censors as they contain lucid details of sexuality and racially justified killing of "foreigners" (i.e. non-Jews), as commanded by "God". Consider theses:

—Jesus says that he wasn't sent with peace on earth but with a sword
    (Matthew 10:34)

—Jesus acts like the Taliban: *"But as for those enemies of mine, who would not have me reign over them, bring them here and slay them before me."* (Luke 19:27)

—Jesus wants division and brings fire: *"I came to cast fire upon the earth; and would that it were already kindled...Do you think that I have come to give peace on earth? No, I tell you, but rather division."* (Luke 12:49-51)

—Jesus is presented as a baby-killer: *"Behold, I will cast her into a bed, and them that commit adultery with her into great tribulation, except they repent of their deeds. And I will kill her children with death; and all the churches shall know that I am he who searcheth the reins and hearts: and I will give unto every one of you according to your works." (Revelation 2:22-23)*

—PSALMS 144:1 God is praised as the one who trains hands for war and fingers for battle.

—2KINGS 2:23-24 Forty-two children are mauled and killed, presumably according to the will of God, for having jeered at a man of God.

—2KINGS 5:27 Elisha curses Gehazi and his descendants forever with leprosy.

—2KINGS 6:29 *"So we cooked my son and ate him. The next day I said to her, 'Give up your son so we may eat him,' but she had hidden him."*

—2KINGS 9:30-37 Jehu has Jezebel killed. Horses trample her body. Dogs eat her flesh so that only her skull, feet, and the palms of her hands remain.

—2KINGS 10:7 Jehu has Ahab's seventy sons beheaded, then sends the heads to their father.

—2KINGS 10:14 Jehu has forty-two of Ahab's kin killed.

—2KINGS 10:17 "And when he came to Samaria, he slew all that remained to Ahab in Samaria, till he had wiped them out, according to the word of the Lord ...."

—2KINGS 10:19-27 Jehu uses trickery to massacre the Baal worshippers.

—2KINGS 14:5, 7 Amaziah kills his servants and then 10,000 Edomites.

—2KINGS 15:3-5 Even though he did what was right in the eyes of the Lord, the Lord smites Azariah with leprosy for not having removed the "high places."

—2KINGS 15:16 Menahem ripped open all the women who were pregnant.

—2KINGS 19:35 An angel of the Lord kills 185,000 men.

—2CHRONICLES 21:4 Jehoram slays all his brothers.

—ISAIAH 49:26 The Lord will cause the oppressors of the Israelite's to eat their own flesh and to become drunk on their own blood as with wine.

—EZEKIEL 6:12-13 The Lord says: *"... they will fall by the sword, famine and plague. He that is far away will die of the plague, and he that is near will fall by the sword, and he that survives and is spared* will die of famine. So will I spend my wrath upon them. And they will know I am the Lord, when the people lie slain among their idols around their altars, on every high hill and on all the mountaintops, under every spreading tree and every leafy oak...."

—EZEKIEL 9:4-6 The Lord commands: "... *slay old men outright, young men and maidens, little children and women....*"

—EZEKIEL 20:26 God commands infanticide? In order that he might horrify them, the Lord allowed the Israelites to defile themselves and amongst other things, *the sacrifice of their firstborn children.*

—EZEKIEL 21:3-4 The Lord says that he will cut off both the righteous and the wicked that his sword shall go against all flesh.

—EZEKIEL 23:25,47 God is going to slay the sons and daughters of those who were whores.

—HOSEA 13:16 The "Lord" says: *"They shall fall by the sword: their infants shall be dashed in pieces, and their women with child shall be ripped up."*

—MATTHEW 11:21-24 Jesus curses [the inhabitants of] three cities who were not sufficiently impressed with his great works.

—Book of Judges 3:29 The Israelites kill about 10,000 Moabites.

—BOOK OF JUDGES 3:31 (A restatement.) Shamgar killed 600 Philistines with an ox-goad.

—BOOK OF JUDGES 4:21 Jael takes a tent stake and hammers it through the head of Sisera, fastening it to the ground.

—BOOK OF JUDGES 7:19-25 The Gideons defeat the Midianites, slay their princes, cut off their heads, and bring the heads back to Gideon.

—BOOK OF JUDGES 8:15-21 The Gideons slaughter the men of Penuel.

—BOOK OF JUDGES 9:45 Abimalech and his men kill all the people in the city.

—BOOK OF JUDGES 11:29-39 Jepthah sacrifices his beloved daughter, his only child, according to a vow he has made with the Lord.

—BOOK OF JUDGES 14:19 The Spirit of the Lord comes upon a man and causes him to slay thirty men.

—BOOK OF JUDGES 15:15 Samson slays 1000 men with the jawbone of an ass.

—BOOK OF JUDGES 16:27-30 Samson, with the help of the Lord, pulls down the pillars of the Philistine house and causes his own death and that of 3000 other men and women.

—BOOK OF JUDGES 18:27 The Danites slay the quiet and unsuspecting people of Laish.

—BOOK OF JUDGES 20:43-48 The Israelites smite 25,000+ "men of valor" from amongst the Benjamites, "men and beasts and all that they found," and set their towns on fire.

—BOOK OF JUDGES 21:10-12 The "Lord" says: *"... Go and smite the inhabitants of Jabesh-gilead with the edge of the sword and; also the women and little ones.... Every male and every woman that has lain with a male you shall utterly destroy."* They do so and find four hundred young virgins whom they bring back for their own use.

Compare the following statements in the Koran to the Bible:

"And if any of the idolaters seeks of you protection, grant him (her) protection till he hears the words of God, then convey him to his

place of security. That is because they are a folk who know not..(Koran 9:6-8)."

"Fight in the way of God against those who fight against you, but begin not hostilities. Indeed God does not love transgressors (Koran 2:192-193)."

"..So if they hold aloof from you and wage not war against you and offer you peace. God allows you no way against them (Koran 4:90)."

"How is it with you that you do not fight in God's way, when the feeble among the men, women and children are saying, "Our lord, bring us forth from this place whose people are tyrants. O God give us from your presence some protector and helper.'(Koran 4:75-76)."

"There is no compulsion in religion. Truth is clear from falsehood (Koran 2:256)

"You are in no way a tyrant or forcer over them; but warn by the Koran him who fears my threat (Koran 50:45)."

The idea of a *United Nations* working for world peace was actually contained in the Koran, centuries before such an organization came into being. It is thus an idea "borrowed" from the Koran:

"There is no good in much of their secret conferences except, him who enjoins alms giving and kindness and <u>peace making</u> among mankind. Whoever does that seeking the good pleasure of God? God will bestow on him (her) a vast reward (Koran 4:114)."

The Bible & Women:

"When men strive together one with another, and the wife of the one draweth near for to deliver her husband out of the hand of him that smiteth him, and putteth forth her hand, and taketh him by the secrets: then thou shalt cut off her hand, thine eye shall not pity her." (Deuteronomy 25:11-12)

Burning Women:

> "And the daughter of any priest, if she profane herself by playing the whore, she profaneth her father: she shall be burnt with fire." (Leviticus 21:9)

Killing witches:

> "Thou shalt not suffer a witch to live. Whoever lieth with a beast shall surely be put to death. He that sacrificeth unto any god, save to the LORD only, he shall be utterly destroyed." (Exodus 22:18-20)

Birth of a female child makes a woman unclean longer than the birth of a male child does:

> "Speak unto the children of Israel, saying, If a woman have conceived seed, and born a man child: then she shall be unclean seven days; according to the days of the separation for her infirmity shall she be unclean…But if she bear a maid child, then she shall be unclean two weeks, as in her separation: and she shall continue in the blood of her purifying threescore and six days." (Leviticus 12:2-5)

Men rulers and "gods" over women:

> "But I would have you know, that the head of every man is Christ; and the head of the woman is the man; and the head of Christ is God." (New Testament, I Corinthians 11:3)

> "Wives, submit yourselves unto your own husbands, as unto the Lord. For the husband is the head of the wife, even as Christ is the head of the church: and he is the savior of the body. Therefore as the church is subject unto Christ, so let the wives be to their own husbands in everything. " (New Testament, Ephesians 5:22-24)

Women created for man:

> "For the man is not of the woman; but the woman of the man. Neither was the man created for the woman; but the woman for the man." (New, Testament, I Corinthians 11:8-9)

Silencing the woman:

> "Let the women learn in silence with all subjection. But I suffer not a woman to teach, nor to usurp authority over the man, but to be in silence. For Adam was first formed, then Eve. And Adam was not deceived, but the woman being deceived was in the transgression." (New Testament, I Timothy 2:11-14)

"God" wants to stone women and men:

> "If a man be found lying with a woman married to an husband, and a man find her in the city, and lie with her, then ye shall bring them both out unto the gate of that city, and ye shall stone them with stones that they die; the damsel, because she cried not, being in the city; and the man, because he hath humbled his neighbour's wife: so thou shalt put away evil from among you." (Deuteronomy 22:23-24)
> Note: There is no statement on stoning men and women in the Koran. Muslim tradition borrowed this ruling from the Bible. The Koran, which is the source of Islam, contains no such ruling at all! The Islam of the Koran is completely different to the "Islam" practiced by groups like the Taliban.

"God" rips pregnant women and kills infants:

> "Samaria shall become desolate; for she hath rebelled against her God: they shall fall by the sword: their infants shall be dashed in pieces, and their women with child shall be ripped up." (Hosea 13:16)

"God" lifts up skirts according to the Bible:

> *"Look, I am against you!- declares Yahweh Saboath- I shall lift your skirts as high as your face and show your nakedness to the nations, your shame to the kingdoms. I shall pelt you with filth."* (Nahum 3:5-6)

Bible and pornography:

> *"Yet she multiplied her whoredoms, in calling to remembrance the days of her youth, wherein she had played the harlot in the land of Egypt. For she doted upon their paramours, <u>whose flesh is as the flesh of asses, and whose issue is like the issue of horses.</u>"* (Ezekiel 23: 20-21)

> *"and lusted after her paramours there, whose members were like those of donkeys, and whose emission was like that of stallions."* (Ezekiel 23: 21, New Revised Standard Version)

> *"Therefore I will wail and howl, I will go stripped and naked: I will make a wailing like the dragons, and mourning as the owls."* (Micah 1:8)

Contrary to the Bible, the Koran, justly egalitarian in its approach, based on its emphasis on the common origin of men and women (Koran 4:1 etc), doesn't agree with the Bible where the Bible says that women were created "from and for" men nor does it say that women cannot teach nor have authority over men. The Koran also dispels the common myth among other religions in general that a woman is evil by nature and has been created to deceive mankind.

The Koran over 1400 years back gave women the right to property ownership, the right to initiate divorce, the right to legal testimony and the right to earn their livelihood if they so pleased. It emphasized equity and kindness in a marital relationship and gave women an equal right to arbitration to resolve differences with their spouses. An unbiased reading of the Koran clearly reveals that it liberated women long before modern women's rights movements were born (for more information see: **http://women.rationalreality.com)**. Compare what the Bible says to these statements in the Koran:

> *"And among God's signs is this: He created for you mates from amongst yourselves (males as mates for females and vice versa) that you might find tranquillity and peace in them. And he has put love and kindness among you. Herein surely are signs for those who reflect (Koran 30:21)."*

> *"And if you fear a breach between the two (husband and wife), appoint an arbiter from his family and an arbiter from her family." (Koran 4:35)*

> *"And when you men have divorced women, ...then either retain them in kindness if you reconcile, or part with them in kindness. Do not retain them to harm them so that you transgress limits. He who does this has wronged himself (Koran 2:231)."*

> *"O believers! It is not lawful for you to inherit women against their will, nor that you should put restrictions on them, that you might take what you had given them...Consort with them in kindness, for if you hate them, it might happen that you hate something in which God has put much good (Koran 4:19)."*

> *"Women impure for men impure. And men impure for women impure. Women of purity for men of purity, and men of purity for women of purity. These are not affected by what people say. For them is forgiveness and an honorable provision (Koran 24:26)."*

> *"And their Lord has heard them and says: 'I don't let the work of any worker be lost be they male or female. You both proceed one from the other..(Koran 3:195)."*

> *"Indeed, men who submit and women who submit, believing men and believing women, and men who obey and women who obey, and truthful men and truthful women, and men who persevere and women who persevere, and men who are humble and women who are humble, and men who give alms and women who give alms, and men who fast and women who fast, and men who guard their chastity and women who guard their chastity, and men who remember God much and women who remember God much. God has prepared for them forgiveness and a great reward (Koran 33:35)."*

> *"And the believers men and women are friends one of the other, they enjoin what is right and forbid what is wrong, and they establish worship and pay the poor due, and they obey God and his messenger. As for these, God will have mercy on them...(Koran 9:71)."*

Women are presented as examples for both men and women, in the Koran:

> *" God cites an <u>example</u> for those who believe: the wife of Pharaoh when she said: My Lord! Build for me a home with you in the Garden, and deliver me from Pharaoh and his work and save me from a tyrannous people. And Mary the daughter, who guarded her chastity, and we inspired in her of our spirit. She confirmed the words of her God and his books and was of the steadfast (Koran 66: 11-12)."*

The Prophets (according to the Bible):

Abraham married his sister (Genesis 20:12)

Lot had incest with his daughters who begat his children (Genesis 19:30)

David had adultery with Bathsheba (2 Samuel 11:1-7)

Solomon worshipped idols (1 Kings 11:4)

Noah was a drunkard and lay naked in his intoxication (Genesis 9:20)

Aaron led people to worship the golden calf (Exodus 32:2-11)

Jesus was seen as a wine bibber (Matthew 11:19; Luke 7:34)

Jacob was a deceiver (Genesis 27)

Alcohol dependency and the Bible:

> *Proverbs 31:6-7 "Give strong drink to him who is ready to perish, and wine to those that be of heavy hearts. Let him drink and forget his poverty and remember his misery no more."*

Or this contradiction:

> *Proverbs 20:1 (just 11 chapters earlier):"Wine is a mocker, strong drink is a raging and whomsoever is deceived thereby is not wise."*

Compare this to the Koran's "scientific" conclusion regarding alcohol:

> *"They ask you concerning intoxicants (Alcohol and other Drugs)...Say: In them is great harm and some benefits for humankind. But the harm of them is much greater than their benefit (Koran 2:219)*

The Food and Drug Administration (FDA) in the United States, uses the criterion of the Koran, given in the above statement, when it tests any new innovative drug. If the harm or side effects of any drug are found to exceed their usefulness, they are banned from further production and marketing.

Conclusion:

The Koran, in establishing itself as being the word of an all-knowing God, presented a scientific test of falsification regarding books that claim to be from God. It stated:

> *"Do they not consider the Koran with care. If it had been from anyone other than God, it would contain many contradictions."*
> *(Koran 4:82)*

This "industry" of manufacturing the "word of God" was in vogue in ancient times when religion was the most powerful institution in society. Thus the elite whenever they wanted to convince people of something, to further their economic gain, used religion. This not only distorted and ruined the genuine "words of God", it created mischief and corruption in society which ultimately got blamed on religion. It was not religion but pseudo-religion and constructed books, like parts of the Bible, that got institutionalized and caused great harm and injustice to humanity. The Koran, coming to reform such a world, presented itself as a criterion to distinguish true from false (Koran 2:185), based on the principles of science and rationality. It termed nature as being the reflections of God's will (*Sunna* in Arabic). It termed the careful analysis of nature and contemplation based on it, as a duty for every believer (Koran 3:195). The history of modern science began with the Koran. Muslims inspired by the Koran did pioneering foundation building work in all fields of modern science, thus sparking the European Renaissance.

The Koran knew that pseudo-religion was harmful, so it termed telling lies about God the greatest wrong anyone could do. The Book of Jeremiah in the Old Testament of the Bible, regarded by many Jewish scholars as being the "most authentic" of all books of the Bible, clearly states how scribes deliberately lie with their pen to convince people of certain things that they falsely manufacture, being from God when they are in fact not:

"How can you say that we are wise and that the law of the lord is with us but behold, the false pen of the scribe has made it into a lie." (The Bible, Jeremiah 8:8)

"Let there be no compulsion in religion. Truth is clearly distinct from falsehood." (Koran 2:256)

Sources:

Asadi, Muhammed. 1989. *Islam or Christianity?* Karachi, Pakistan.
Deedat, Ahmed. *Is the Bible God's Word?* IPCI, South Africa.
Miller, Gary. *A Concise Reply to Christianity.*
Other sources are acknowledged within the text for clarity.

2

JESUS IN THE KORAN & THE BIBLE:

IS JESUS GOD?

"...Such was Jesus, the son of Mary. A statement of truth, about which they dispute."
—*(Koran 19:34)*

The main difference between Islam and Christianity revolves around the divinity of Christ. Whereas the Koran states that Jesus was no more than a prophet of God, a human being, Christian doctrine insists that he was in some way divine, a son of God. The doctrine of God incarnate, whereby it is implied that that "word" that was divine became flesh, is central to almost all denominations of Christianity.

The concept of the Trinity, popular among the majority of Christian churches embodies within itself the notion that three distinct co-equals are God. The Koran on the other hand states unequivocally, that God is just one (indivisible) and that no one can be held equal to God (Koran 112:1-4). This absolute oneness of God forms the very heart and soul of the system called Islam. The Christian articles of God-Incarnate, Son of God, and Holy Trinity, clearly violate the oneness of God embodied in Islam.

In any logical and scientific study of religion, it is necessary to consider the facts and then go to the origin of the problem, as opposed to just dealing with the subjective claims of the followers of the various systems. The standard for Islam is the Koran, that for Christianity is the Bible particularly the New Testament. Therefore, let us go to the sources and examine them to see if there is conflict or conciliation.

As a Muslim is writing this document, it is understood that the majority of people belonging to the "other camp" will be skeptical as to the intentions and purpose of this research. For this reason, it is request that the style of the document be considered, which will hopefully show that value judgments have been avoided and that the arguments and quotations are stated clearly and truthfully. If however it is still believed that some information has been presented incorrectly or misquoted from the source books, it is requested that corrections be sent to the author for comments and consideration and possible change of stand on issues.

THE TRINITY:

The *Athnasian Creed* formalized the concept of the Holy Trinity. In its standard form, the wording runs as follows:

> "There is one person of the Father, another of the Son, and another of the Holy Ghost. But the Godhead of the Father, and of the Son and of the Holy Ghost is all one, the glory equal, and the majesty co-eternal.... The Father is God, the Son is God, the Holy Ghost is God, and yet there are not three Gods but one God."

GOD INCARNATE:

The concept of "God incarnate" that Christianity embodies in its doctrine, states that God became man, and that man was Jesus. It is claimed that Jesus shared the nature of God in every way and that he was in every way a God, and a man. He was the only "begotten" Son of God and hence a *"Son of God"* in a *unique* fashion, unlike anyone else.

Logic and the Trinity:

From the standpoint of mathematics and the English language, when we say that this is a person, that is another person and that that one is yet another, it is understood that there are three people involved and not just one. One plus one plus one will always be three and not one, no matter how it is put. Therefore, the concept of Trinity is itself faulty, logically speaking. If the three are separately and distinctly God then there are three distinct Gods, according to the language. If there is only one God, then each, Father, Son and Holy Ghost, on their own cannot be God but only parts of God. Yet God is supposed to be indivisible!

From the standpoint of the human mind's comprehension, when the preacher says, "In the name of the Father," a certain distinct mental image or idea emerges. When he continues, "And the Son", the idea or image that one gets now is different. The same is the case when the preacher utters the words Holy Ghost. No matter how hard you try; you can never super-impose these three distinct pictures as one. When the "Son" is mentioned, most Christians see a Jesus, whatever image of him is popular in the culture, when the "Holy Ghost" is mentioned, the picture changes. Three persons can never be one person. One person can have parts to his/her personality. Together those parts form the person. However, the concept of the Trinity states it completely different. It is claimed that Jesus is not a part of God but 100% God on his own, so also the Holy Ghost and the Father. But then it is concluded that they are not three but one God. The premise of the statement does not support its conclusion about there being one God. It makes the assertion about the Trinity impossible to prove logically and reduces it to just words, which can not have any logical meaning.

Jesus, according to the source of Christianity, in the records that we have of his sayings, never made a claim to be divine. In an answer to a question on what the first commandment was, he replied, *"The First is, "Hear O Israel, the Lord our God is One (Mark 12:29)."*

The word translated "one" in the above verse is the Hebrew <u>*Ikhad*</u>. This word is the same as the Arabic <u>*Ahad*</u>. It means one whole, indivisible. It does not and cannot in anyway represent the Trinity but rather it disqualifies it. It is well documented and understood by scholars of the history of Christianity, universally, that the Trinity was a later invention, and was never preached by Jesus. Jesus talked about the one God and His kingdom.

When the believers in the divinity of Christ are asked about whether Jesus himself ever made a claim to be God, in the sources that they have, a handful of basically similar references across the board, are offered to the questioner. However, all of these references when studied in their context and in the context of other explicit statements made by Jesus, fail to prove that Jesus was claiming to be God in any way.

There are three main problems with the claims that are presented. They are either i) insufficient on their own to prove the divinity of any person, ii) or it is impossible, on the basis of the verse alone to prove the divinity of any person, or iii) They are ambiguous; in that they are open to alternative interpretations which are as valid as what is asserted.

THE CLAIMS:

Claim 1. Jesus says, "I and the Father are One (John 10:30)."

It is claimed on the basis of the above quotation (which is almost always presented without its context) that Jesus was claiming equality with God. The problem with this assertion is that the context has been taken out, either deliberately or out of ignorance. My experience with people presenting this claim is that they are often unaware of where the quotation came from in the Gospel of John.

Beginning at verse 23 of the Gospel of John, chapter 10 we read (in the context of 10:30) about Jesus talking to the Jews. In verse 28, talking about his followers as his sheep, he states:

> "...Neither shall any man pluck them out of my hand. 29) My Father, who gave them me, is greater than all, and no man is able to pluck them out of my Father's hand. 30) I and the Father are one." (John 10:28-30)

The above verses proves only that Jesus and the Father are one in that no man can pluck the sheep out of either's hand. It does not at all state that Jesus is God's equal in everything. In fact the words of Jesus, *"My Father, who gave them me is Greater than ALL..."* in the same passage, completely negates this claim, otherwise we are left with a contradiction. "All" includes everyone, even Jesus.

In the 17th chapter of John, verses 20-22, the same word ONE used in the above verses, in the Greek, i.e. <u>*HEN*</u> is used, not only to describe Jesus and the Father but to describe Jesus, the Father and eleven of the twelve disciples of Jesus. So here if that implies equality, we have a unique case of 13 Gods.

> *"That the ALL may be made <u>ONE</u>. Like thou Father art in me, I in thee, that they may be ONE in us. I in them, they in me, that they may be perfect in ONE (John 17:20-22)."*

Of the verse in question, *"I and the Father are One (John 10:30),"* we also need to take note of the verses following the 30th verse in the passage. In those verses, the Jews accuse Jesus falsely of claiming to be God by these words. He however replies, proving their accusation wrong by their own Scripture:

> *"The Jews answered him saying, 'For a good work we stone thee not, but for blasphemy, and because that thou being a man, makest thyself a God '(John 10:33)."*

Jesus replies to this accusation saying:

> *"Jesus answered them, 'Is it not written in your Law, "I said ye are gods." If He can call them gods, unto whom the word of God came, say ye of him whom the Father hath sanctified and sent into the world, "Thou blasphemeth," because I said I am the son of God?' (John 10:34-36)."*

In the language of the Bible, in *Psalms 82* from which Jesus quotes above, the word "gods" is used by God to describe the prophets *("to whom the word of God came")*. Jesus argues with the Jews that if God can call the prophets "gods", then his saying that he is the "son of God," is no claim to divinity, just as the other prophets were not God just because they were referred to as gods by God himself.

The point that Jesus makes to the Jews is further proven by the use of the term "Son of God," in both the Old and the New Testament. Metaphorically speaking, God is the cherisher and sustainer and hence the "Father" of everybody. This doesn't mean that the person so described as a "Son of God" is physically begotten by God or of the same nature as God or literally the "son" as humans have biological sons. Otherwise the term "son of God" would not make any sense.

God does not beget:

God by definition signifies one who received his existence from nobody, whereas son signifies someone who received his existence from somebody else. God and son are mutually exclusive terms, they cannot go together. The use of the term by Jesus, and in other places in the Bible is metaphoric and not literal. If God is like a human being in that he begets sons which are "like" him in nature then we cannot resolve the question, "Who created God?", that the atheist asks. The atheist asks this question because of his preconception of a Christian God, the Father who begets children.

Empirical evidence provided by nature, suggests that an intelligent being created the heavens and the earth. This being however cannot be "human" or like anything in the natural world, so to speak. The attributes of the universe that "necessitate" design, as well as the attributes in us that "necessitate" design cannot be the attributes of a creator otherwise "it" would need a creator as well.

Thus, if the creator is "different" than creation, in the attributes that "it" possesses, the question "Who created God?" becomes logically meaningless. Intelligent design would apply only to things that were non-existent and then came into being and contain specific attributes that necessitate design. Thus God has to be eternal, unchanging and unlike creation:

> *"God is the cleaver of the skies and the earth. He has made pairs of yourself and the animals, whereby he multiplies you. Nothing is as His example..."(Koran 42:11)*

The many "sons" of God in the Bible:

1. Luke 3:38 *"...Adam which was the Son of God."*

2. Genesis 6:2 &4 *"That the sons of God saw the daughters of men...and when the sons of God came in unto the daughters of men..."*

3. Exodus 4:22 *"Israel is my son even my first born."*

4. Romans 8:14 *"For as many as are led by the spirit of God are called sons of God,"*

5. Matthew 5:9 *"Blessed are the peace-makers for they shall be called sons of God."*

By the above quotations from the Bible it should be clear that the term "Son of God," signifies only a righteous person. It does not mean that the person so titled is divine, or we would have hundreds of Gods according to the Bible. Jesus is described as the "son of man," 83 times in the New Testament whereas he's described only 13 times as the Son of God. What we also see is that Jesus used the terms, "Your Father,"

"Thy Father," describing God's relationship with people 13 times before the first time he ever said, "My Father," about God. All these show that he was in no way implying that God physically begot him or he was unique as a "Son of God".

It is claimed that in John 3:16 (the favorite verse of the evangelists) that Jesus is referred to as the only Son of God. A careful reading of the verse compared to *Hebrews 11:17* shows that Isaac is described as the only son of Abraham, whereas literally speaking Isaac was never the only son of Abraham as Ishmael was born before him. The use of the word is metaphoric; Jesus was special among the sons of God but certainly not unique or begotten.

Peter in the Book of Acts testifies about Jesus:

> *"O you men of Israel, hear these words: Jesus of Nazareth, a MAN approved of God among you…(Acts 2:22)."*

Jesus thus even to his disciples, as to early Christians, not poisoned by Pauline doctrine, was a man, not a God.

Claim 2) Jesus was Immanuel, i.e. "God with us".

Another claim that is often times made is concerning Isaiah 7:14. In the Book of Isaiah in the Old Testament of the Bible it states:

> *"Therefore, the Lord himself will give you a sign, behold a young woman (almah) will conceive and bear a child and shall call his name Immanuel."*

It is claimed that the above was a prophecy about the birth of Jesus to the Virgin Mary. It is further claimed that since the word Immanuel means "God with us," the person being talked about, i.e. Jesus, was God.

The above quotation is from the King James Version of the Bible. The word translated as "virgin" is the wrong translation of the Hebrew word *ALMAH*. The word *ALMAH* in Hebrew means "young woman." The correct Hebrew word for virgin is *BETHU-LAH*. Since many young women begot children since those words were penned, it is not at all necessary that those words should apply to Jesus.

Another fact that is often ignored is that Jesus was never named Immanuel, nor did anyone ever address him as Immanuel when he lived. On the contrary, the Messiah was named Jesus (*Luke 2:21*) by the angel according to the gospels. Also, even if a person is named Immanuel, it doesn't mean that the person so named is God.

Consider for example all the people named *ELI* in the Old Testament. ELI means God in the Hebrew. It is also narrated that Jesus while talking to God referred to Him as ELI (*Mark 15:34 & Matthew 27:46*). We cannot however on this basis of just a name accept all the people named ELI in the Old Testament as Gods. Similarly, we cannot accept a person named Immanuel (which means "God with us") as God. Jesus was never named Immanuel anyway, so both ways the argument and claim are false.

Claim 3) The word became flesh:

Another common claim is John 1:1 which reads:

"In the beginning was the word, and the word was with God, and the word was God."

This is often presented from the Gospel of John to prove that Jesus was God. There are however several problems with this claim. By the above verse it is assumed that Jesus was the "word" and since the word was God and became flesh, Jesus is God. The statement that John (or whoever wrote this gospel) reproduced in his gospel was uttered not by John but by a certain Philo of Alexandria, years before Jesus or John were born. It is therefore completely unlikely that Philo was even remotely referring to Jesus.

There is also another reason, considering the Greek of the above verse, which disproves the assertion that Jesus is referred to as God in the verse. In the verse above, the first time the word God is used, the Greek is *HOTHEOS*, which means "The God". The second time the word God is used, "and the word was God," the word for God is *TONTHEOS*, which means "A God". Europeans have evolved a system of capital and small letters non-existent in Greek. The God, *HOTHEOS* is translated as God with a capital "G", whereas Tontheos, which means A or ANY God is translated with a small "g", god. In this case however, we see the unlawful translators trying to prove Jesus being God by putting capital "G" for both, whereas it doesn't belong in the case of the "word". Consider these other candidates for "a god" i.e. *Tontheos,* in the Bible:

> *Exodus 7:1 (God said to Moses)"See I have made you <u>a god</u> (in the Greek it would be Tontheos, doesn't mean God almighty but just a god.) to Pharaoh and Aaron thy brother will be thy prophet."*

Consider this statement where the Devil is "The God", i.e. *Hotheos,* but the translators cover it up. In *2 Corinthians 4:4* Paul states that the Devil is the God (should be capital "G" but the translators translate it with a small "g" instead of capital) of the world.

The word "a god", *Tontheos,* in the Bible is used for every other person including the prophets. It does not mean the person is God almighty. As examples consider the above quote from Exodus where Moses is referred to as God and also Psalms 82:6 where God allegedly refers to the prophets as gods:

"I said, Ye are all gods and all of you are the children of the Most High."(Psalms 82:6)

Claim 4) God in the plural?

Another common claim presented from the Bible to "prove" the divinity of Christ is presented surprisingly from the first chapter of the book of Genesis. God supposedly says: *"Let US create."* The word "us" is plural and has been used by God for himself in Genesis. Christians assert that this plural proves the Trinity, otherwise God would have used the singular. This claim is based on ignorance of Semitic languages. In most eastern languages, there are two types of plurals, i.e. plural of numbers and plural of respect. In the Koran, God speaks of Himself as "us" and "we" as well. Yet in those verses, no Muslim will ever doubt that God is referring to Himself alone.

Even in old English, the King or the Queen would use such plurals for themselves alone. An objective inquiry from Jewish scholars, whose book the Old Testament is, will reveal the same. Also, modern translators recognize this and therefore translate the word *ELOHIM* in the Old Testament as God and not Gods even though it is a plural. I have never seen a Bible with the word ELOHIM translated as "Gods". It is a plural of respect; it does not signify the Trinity.

Claim 5) Seeing Jesus is seeing the Father?

Yet another common claim that is presented is Philip's statement in John 14:9 where Philip asks to be shown God, and Jesus replies,

"If you have seen me you have seen the Father." (John 14:9)

By this statement the Christian claims that what Jesus is <u>really</u> saying is that "I am the Father." However, Jesus is not saying this. We need to read the context of the verse in question. Beginning from verse 4, we see that the disciples are misunderstanding Jesus from the beginning. In verse 4, Jesus is talking about a spiritual journey, i.e. going to God, whereas Philip takes it to be a physical journey. In verse 7, Jesus makes clear that to know him would be to know God since Jesus was conveying knowledge about God. Philip then asks Jesus to show them the Father to which the response in 14:9 comes. Since God cannot be seen according to the law of the Jews (which says that *No one can see God and live*), the only way that He can be known is through His signs and messengers. Therefore, Jesus' response *"If you have seen me you have seen the Father,"* is consistent with this. He is not claiming to be God.

However, to further prove that Jesus was not claiming to be God, consider what Jesus says in *John 5:32*:

> "You have not heard him (God) at any time NEITHER seen His shape or form."

Now the Jews and the disciples were seeing Jesus. If Jesus was God then this statement by him is a gross error and a contradiction compared to John14: 9. However, to the contrary, Jesus says:

i) *"The Father is greater than I." John 14:28*
ii) *"The Father is greater than ALL." (John 10:29)*
iii) *" I can of mine own self do NOTHING…I seek not my own will but the will of Him **who sent** me (John 5:30)."*
iv) *"… **the one who is sent** is not greater than the one who sent (John 13:16)."*

God according to Judaism, Christianity and Islam has knowledge of everything. Jesus according to the Gospels had limited knowledge and therefore can not be God:

> "For of that hour (of Judgment) knows no man, no not the angels, NEITHER THE SON, but the Father in heaven (John 10:32)."

A similar event is documented in Mark 11: 12-13 where Jesus appears ignorant of the season of fruiting of the fig tree.

Claim 6) Jesus raised the dead?

In trying to prove the divinity of Jesus, Christians assert that Jesus gave life to the dead, something that only God can do and hence he was God. The major problem with this assertion is the continual denial on the part of Jesus that he was doing the miracles on his own. In John 5:30 above, for example, we read that Jesus disclaims having the power to do anything. In Matthew 28:18 it is further asserted that all power to do everything was *GIVEN* to Jesus. In this context, read John 12:49. Hence Jesus is the receiver (recipient) and not the originator of that power. A reading of John 11:40-43, which tells the story of the bringing back of Lazarus to life, clearly shows that it was God who brought Lazarus back to life, using Jesus:

> *"Then he took away the stone from the place the dead was laid; and Jesus lifted up his eyes and said: 'Father, <u>I thank thee that thou hast heard me</u>, and I know that you hear me always....'* (John 11:40-43)

God heard Jesus, and Jesus knew that God would work the miracle through him.

Claim 7) Jesus had no father:

The Koran and the New Testament both suggest that Jesus was born without a father and only had a mother. This is sometimes presented by Christians to prove that God was the father of Jesus in a physical sense and hence Jesus was God the son or the Son of God.

The Koran clarifies this misconception by comparing the creation of Jesus to the creation of Adam (Koran 3:59). God, who created the first humans could create a man without a father. It is no big deal for God. Modern science can theoretically do the same using just the egg of the female through cloning. The New Testament points to another man also, born without a father or mother; a greater feat than Jesus, who is not God. Consider this passage in the Bible, New Testament:

> *"For this Melchizedec, King of Salem, priest of the Most High God.... <u>Without father, without mother,</u> without genealogy, having neither beginning of days or end of life...."* (Hebrews 7:1-3)

Can anyone match that? Therefore, it is insufficient on the basis of the above alone to prove that a person was God just because he had no father. According to the Christian assumptions about God, He has no shape or sex (see John 4:24), but Jesus had a human form and was of the male gender (Luke 2:21). Therefore, Jesus cannot be God. God has no beginning or end. Jesus had a beginning (Luke 2:6) and according to Christianity, a violent death on the cross. Therefore he cannot be God.

Claim 8: "My God and my Lord"?

It is often claimed that since Thomas referred to Jesus *as "My God, my Lord" (John 20:28)*, that Jesus was God. An ignorance of the context of the verse and of Christian doctrine prompts this claim. The context of the verse talks about an unbelieving Thomas being surprised when Jesus offers him evidence. The exclamation, "My God," on his part was just astonishment. We use such an exclamation everyday while talking to people (abbreviated as OMG). This doesn't mean that the person we are talking to is God. For example, I see John cutting his wrist with a *Rambo* knife. I say: "My God, John what are you doing?" Do I mean that John is God? Similar is the use of the expression by Thomas. If you go into Jewish or Muslim societies even today, you'll hear people exclaim "My God, my Lord," at every situation which surprises them or causes them anguish or is astonishing.

In the verse above Thomas says: *"My God, my Lord,"* he was not claiming that Jesus was his 1) God and 2) Lord. If he did then the Church should have stamped him a heretic right. That is because claiming that Jesus is *Lord and God* is a violation of Christian doctrine, which asserts that there is one God, the Father and one Lord, Jesus. Jesus can't be God and Lord.

"...Yet for us there is but one God, the Father...and one Lord, Jesus Christ."
(I Corinthians 8:)

Believing the above (i.e. Jesus is Lord and God) would leave a person with unorthodox doctrine branded by the Church *as Sabellianism, Patripassianism, or Monarchianism.*

Claim 9) "I am"!

It is claimed that Jesus used the words, "I am", and since these same words were used by God to describe Himself to the people in the Old Testament, Jesus was claiming to be God. John 8:58, is presented to back this claim. In the verse, Jesus says*:" Before Abraham was I am."*

Now, if Jesus existed before Abraham did, that might be a remarkable thing, but does that prove that he was God? How many people existed before Abraham? The Bible presents Jeremiah as being a prophet before he was conceived in his mother's womb (Jeremiah 1:5), yet no one says that his pre-human existence qualifies him for being a claimant to deity.

In Exodus chapter 3, God allegedly says: *"I am what I am."* Long before the time of Jesus, there existed a Greek translation of the Old Testament called the Septuagint. The key word, "I am," in Exodus, which is used by Christians to prove the deity of Jesus is translated as *"HO ON."* However, when Jesus uses the word in John 8:58, the Greek of the "I am," is *EGO EIMI*. If Jesus wanted to tell the Jews that he was claiming to be God he should have at least remained consistent in the use of words or the whole point is lost. How many people in that age would have said, "I am," in answer to questions in everyday life, hundreds of thousands. Are they all gods? If you ask me: "Are you Asadi," and I say "I am," am I claiming to be God just because God happened to use the words "I am?" The argument clearly is not valid.

Claim 10) ABBA, father

It is sometimes claimed that the use of the Hebrew word for father, ABBA, by Jesus for God, signifies a special "son" relationship of a physical type. This however is unwarranted since every Christian is supposed to use the same word ABBA for God (see Romans 8:14, and Galatians 4:6)

Sometimes, certain other terms used by Jesus for himself are presented to prove that he was claiming divinity. Terms like "Messiah," and "Savior," are not only applied to Jesus in the gospels but have been applied to others in the Bible. Yet in their case, no one says that they prove divinity. If these claims were to be presented truthfully then we would have not one but many candidates for divinity.

As examples, Cyrus the Persian, who was a pagan is called Messiah in the Bible (Isaiah 45:1). It is however covered up by the translators who translate the word as anointed. The Hebrew and the Arabic word Messiah comes from the root *Masaaha*, which means to rub, message or anoint. Ancient kings and priests were "anointed" or appointed, into office. It does not mean that the person so named and termed is God at all. The title of "savior," or "saviors" is used for other people in the Bible (2 Kings 13:5 and Obadiah 21 and Nehemiah 9:27). Translators are well aware of this so they substitute the word savior for deliverer to throw off readers.

Jesus had a servant-master relationship with God. He never claimed to be equal to God, or to be of the same nature as God. Attributing divinity to Christ, a man, goes completely against his teachings as found in the New Testament of the Bible. He says for example that God was his God as well:

> "And go and tell my brethren that I ascend to My Father and Your Father, to MY GOD and your God (John 20:17)."

The Koran confirms this statement made by Jesus:

> *"Indeed they reject the truth, those that say, "God is Christ, the son of Mary." For indeed, Christ said, worship God, who is MY GOD and your God (Koran 5:75)."*

Historical analysis confirms the Koran:

> *"In their relentless search for "the historical Jesus," various Biblical Scholars argue that the Gospel stories of the empty tomb and Jesus' post-resurrection appearances are fictions devised long after his death to justify claims of his divinity." (Rethinking the Resurrection, Newsweek. April 8 1996, page 42)*

> *"While believers through the ages have echoed Peter's faith-filled declaration, "You are the Christ, the Son of the living God," some modern scholars say that historical evidence reveals a much different portrait of Jesus than the one in Christian creeds." (In search of Jesus, U.S. News & World Report, April 8 1996, page 47)*

> *"He (Jesus) was nothing but a mortal servant (of God), on whom We bestowed favor, and made him an example-setter for the Children of Israel." (Koran 43:59)*

Christianity and its view of Muhammed:

Whereas Islam honors Jesus as a great prophet of God and mentions his mother Mary as being *"chosen above the women of all nations,"* Christianity has harbored hate and contempt for Muhammed, the messenger of Allah, throughout history. Consider this summary by Greever (**http://people.ucsc.edu/~slugbug/muhammad.doc**, retrieved 12/01/'01):

> "The famous Christian monk, John of Damascus, showed a complete lack of respect for Muhammad when he wrote of him as a "false prophet", calling his pronouncements "heresy" and "worthy of laughter" (as quoted. in Phipps 3). In the twelfth century, Peter the Venerable wrote:

Muhammad, instructed by the best Jewish and heretical doctors, produced his Quran and wove together, in that barbarous fashion of his, a diabolical scripture put together both from the Jewish fables and the trifling songs of heretics. Lying that his collection was brought to him chapter by chapter by Gabriel, whose name he already knew from the standard Scripture, he poisoned with a deadly poison the people that did not know God. (as quoted. in Phipps 4)

Thomas Aquinas, the Catholic theologian, not only insulted Muhammad but his followers as well when he wrote,

"The truths that he taught he mingled with many fables and with doctrine of the greatest falsity… Those who believed in him were brutal men and desert wanderers, utterly ignorant of all divine teaching, through whose numbers Muhammad forced others to become his followers by the violence of his arms" (as quoted. in Phipps 5).

The Protestant Martin Luther likened Muhammad to:

"The warring horses of the Book of Revelation that bring great destruction to Christians", described him as "course and filthy" (as quoted. in Phipps 6),

And,

"With the maturity of a child called him "an uncouth blockhead and ass" (as quoted. in Phipps 5).

Martin Luther also wrote that:

"the spirit of lies had taken possession of Mohammed, and the devil had murdered men's souls with his Koran and had destroyed the faith of Christians"(as quoted. in Phipps 5-6),

"We are fighting that the Turk may not put his devilish filth and blasphemous Muhammad in the place of our dear Lord, Jesus Christ" (as quoted. in Phipps 6), once again associating Muhammad with lies, the devil, and destruction.

Clearly, it is not Islam that seeks conflict with Christianity, rather Christianity's "holy men" seek conflict with Islam by insults and *Ad Hominem* arguments against Muhammed.

Sources:

Asadi, Muhammed. *Islam & The Divinity of Christ. (1989, revised)*
Deedat, Ahmed. *Is Jesus God.*
Miller, Gary. *A Concise Reply to Christianity.*
Phipps, William E. *Muhammad and Jesus.* New York: The Continuum Publishing Company, 1996. (as cited at **http://people.ucsc.edu/~slugbug/muhammad.doc)**

3

PAUL AND THE INVENTION OF CHRISTIANITY

On the road to Damascus, while persecuting the early Christians, after the death of Jesus, a man claimed that he saw a vision, a vision of Jesus. The man was Saul of Tarsus (Latinized as Paul). From there on, the teachings of Christ were transformed and Romanized and modern Christianity was born.

The vision in which Paul claims that Jesus gave him an authority to teach in his name is recorded a number of times in the New Testament. If we were to analyze these variant descriptions, made by the same man, as in a court of law, they would be thrown out as fabricated "evidence" because of inconsistencies. For example:

1. Acts (9:3-7)

[3] Now as he journeyed he approached Damascus, and suddenly a light from heaven flashed about him.
[4] And <u>he fell to the ground</u> and heard a voice saying to him, "Saul, Saul, why do you persecute me?"
[5] And he said, "Who are you, Lord?" And he said, "I am Jesus, whom you are persecuting;
[6] but rise and enter the city, and you will be told what you are to do."

[7] The men who were traveling with him stood speechless, <u>hearing the voice but seeing no one.</u>

In this description, it is stated that only Paul fell to the ground. And, the other men who traveled with him did not see anything but heard a voice. Compare this to the next description:

2. Acts (22:6-9)

[6] "As I made my journey and drew near to Damascus, about noon a great light from heaven suddenly shone about me.
[7] And I fell to the ground and heard a voice saying to me, `Saul, Saul, why do you persecute me?'
[8] And I answered, `Who are you, Lord?' And he said to me, `I am Jesus of Nazareth whom you are persecuting.'
[9] Now those who were with <u>me saw the light but did not hear the voice</u> of the one who was speaking to me.

In this description, in complete contradiction to the one above, Paul states that those who traveled with him did not hear the voice but saw the light. The previous description said that they did not see anything but heard a voice!

3. Acts (26:14)

[14] And when we had all fallen to the ground, I heard a voice saying to me in the Hebrew language, `Saul, Saul, why do you persecute me? It hurts you to kick against the goads.'

In this description, Paul says that they "all" fell to the ground whereas in the previous description, only Paul had fallen to the ground.

In any court of law, anywhere in the world where justice is upheld, this testimony of Paul would have been thrown out as fabrication and he would have been persecuted for perjury.

Paul's Christianity is not what Jesus taught:

The German philosopher, Fredrick Neitzsche recognized Paul's role in constructing the "new" Christianity, and was convinced of deception:

> *In Nietzsche's view, the very worst of them was Paul, the actual founder of the Christian church and doctrine. Nietzsche was convinced that Paul was not sincere in his beliefs, that "his requirement was power." Nietzsche cannot bring himself to believe that Paul, "whose home was the principal center of Stoic enlightenment," is sincere when he offers up a hallucination as proof that The Redeemer still lives. Paul invented the doctrines of 'eternal life' and 'the Judgement' as a means to his ends. In Die Morgenrote (translated by R. J. Hollingdale as Daybreak, Cambridge Univ. Press, 1982), Nietzsche had earlier discussed Paul's frustrations at being unable to master, and to comply with, Jewish law, and hence Paul "sought about for a means of destroying" that law. Christianity offered Paul just the weapon he had been seeking. [A 40-42; Die Morgenrote 68,* **http://www.debunker.com/texts/anti_chr.html**, *retrieved 12/08/'01].*

Paul destroyed the Law:

Romans 3:28

> *[28] For we hold that a man is justified by faith apart from works of law.*

Romans 7:4

[4] Likewise, my brethren, you have died to the law through the body of Christ, so that you may belong to another, to him who has been raised from the dead in order that we may bear fruit for God.

1 Corinthians 10:25

[25] Eat whatever is sold in the meat market without raising any question on the ground of conscience.

Contrary to what Paul taught, Jesus stated that he came to fulfil the Law and not abolish it. He further states that whoever takes the least bit out of the Law will be "the least" in the Kingdom of Heaven. Since Paul took the "whole" law out, according to Jesus' criteria, Paul is the "least" of the "least"! Consider these words of Jesus:

Matthew 5:17-20:

[17] "Think not that I have come to abolish the law and the prophets; I have come not to abolish them but to fulfil them.
[18] For truly, I say to you, till heaven and earth pass away, not an iota, not a dot, will pass from the law until all is accomplished.
[19] Whoever then relaxes one of the least of these commandments and teaches men so, shall be called least in the kingdom of heaven; but he who does them and teaches them shall be called great in the kingdom of heaven.
[20] For I tell you, unless your righteousness exceeds that of the scribes and Pharisees, you will never enter the kingdom of heaven. "

The Law laid down strict dietary laws, for example, the Book of Deuteronomy, a part of the Torah, states:

And the swine, because it parts the hoof but does not chew the cud, is unclean for you. Their flesh you shall not eat, and their carcasses you shall not touch. (Deuteronomy 14:8)

Furthermore, the concept of salvation that Paul brought into Christianity from Greek myth was also alien to what Jesus taught. According to Paul, believing in the "lord" Jesus and confessing that he was raised from the dead, saves a person. He says:

Romans 10:9

> *[9] "Because, if you confess with your lips that <u>Jesus is Lord</u> and believe in your heart that God <u>raised him from the dead</u>, you will be saved. "*

1 Corinthians 15:14:

> *[14] If Christ has not been raised, then our preaching is in vain and your faith is in vain*

This is unequivocally against what Jesus himself taught. Christians need to ask themselves here, "Whom do we believe, Paul or Jesus?" Jesus says explicitly:

Matthew 7:21-23

> *[21] "Not every one who says to me, `<u>Lord, Lord,</u>' shall enter the kingdom of heaven, but he who does the will of my Father who is in heaven.*
> *[22] On that day many will say to me, `<u>Lord, Lord,</u> did we not prophesy in your name, and cast out demons in your name, and do many mighty works in your name?'*
> *[23] And then will I declare to them, `I never knew you; <u>depart from me, you evildoers.</u>'*

Matthew 19:17

> *[17] And he said to him, "Why do you ask me about what is good? One (God) there is who is good. If you would enter life, <u>keep the commandments.</u>"*

James, who knew Jesus much closer than Paul says:

James 2:26

> *[26] For as the body apart from the spirit is dead, so <u>faith apart from works is dead.</u>*

The Original Sin:

Christianity and Islam differ regarding the concept of the Original Sin. According to Christianity, Adam and Eve, the first humans sinned when they ate the forbidden fruit. They were expelled from heaven and sin entered the world. Every child of Adam, you and I, according to Christianity has inherited this sin (as genetic inheritance). Therefore, every male and female is born stained with sin and is therefore destined to hell, from birth. This belief in Christianity gave rise to the doctrine of *Atonement*. According to this doctrine, God sacrificed his "only begotten" son, Jesus to wash away the sins of the world. The only thing people have to do to wash away their hereditary stain is to believe in Jesus as God's son and that he died for them.

Islam does not agree with all this. According to the Koran, every one is responsible for their own doings and nobody can carry the burden of another. God is forgiving and if a person sincerely repents, amends and does what is good and righteous, God forgives. Adam did not ask us before eating the fruit, so how can we be blamed?

In any society, where justice is one of the highest valued morals, killing an innocent man (Jesus) to wash away the sins of the guilty would be condemned as immoral, yet billions of people rejoice over this "gift" of injustice! Once again, the source of conflict is Paul and not Jesus. Jesus never talked about atonement or a "free-ride" through the blood of an innocent man. On the contrary he said, *"...If you would enter life, keep the commandments"* (Matthew 19:17).

It was Paul who brought the concept of the *Original Sin* into Christianity. He says:

Romans 5:12

[12] "Therefore, as sin came into the world through ONE man.."

1 Corinthians 15:21-22

[21] "For as by a man came death (sin), by a man also has come the resurrection of the dead.
[22] For as in Adam all die, so also in Christ shall all be made alive."

As we saw above, Jesus contradicts Paul. Not only that, the Old Testament contradicts Paul as well:

Ezekiel 18:20-22

[20] The soul that sins shall die. The <u>son shall not suffer for the iniquity of the father</u>, nor the father suffer for the iniquity of the son; the righteousness of the righteous shall be upon himself, and the wickedness of the wicked shall be upon himself.
[21] "But if a wicked man turns away from all his sins which he has committed and keeps all my statutes and does what is lawful and right, he shall surely live; he shall not die.
[22] None of the transgressions which he has committed shall be remembered against him; for the righteousness which he has done he shall live.

2 Chronicles 25:4

[4] But he did not put their children to death, according to what is written in the law, in the book of Moses, where the LORD commanded, "The fathers shall not be put to death for the children, or the children be put to death for the fathers; but every man shall die for his own sin."

Major Yeats Brown, in his book, *Life of a Bengal Lancer*, summarized the concept of atonement in Christianity. He states:

"No heathen tribe has conceived so grotesque an idea, involving as it does the assumption, that man was born with a hereditary stain upon him: and that this stain (for which he was not personally responsible) was to be atoned for; and the creator of all things had

to sacrifice his only begotten son, to neutralize this mysterious curse."

Paul actually transformed the strict monotheism that Jesus proclaimed into a religion that is closer to Greek mythology, than it is towards either Judaism or Islam. Things like the "only begotten son", atonement for the sins of humanity etc. were all alien to the strict monotheism of Abraham, Jesus, Muhammad and all the prophets of Israel.

John H. Randall, emeritus professor of philosophy at Columbia University, wrote:

> *"Christianity, at the hands of Paul, became a mystical system of redemption, much like the cult of Isis, and the other sacramental or mystery religions of the day"*
>
> *(Hellenistic Ways of Deliverance and the Making of the Christian Synthesis, 1970, p. 154,* **http://www.leaderu.com/everystudent/easter/articles/yama.html***, retrieved 12/0-8/'01).*

Greek cults were prevalent in the Mediterranean long before Jesus was born. They were brought into Christianity by Paul to make doctrine "inclusive" thereby destroying the strict monotheism that Jesus proclaimed. Some of the ones, with their parallels in Christianity, are:

1. *Attis of Phrygia (later called Galatia in Asia Minor):*

   He was regarded as the "only begotten" son and savior. He was bled to death on March 24th on the foot of a pine tree. He also rose from the dead and his death and resurrection was celebrated by his followers.

   > *"A Christian writer of the fourth century AD, recounted ongoing disputes between Pagans and Christians over the remarkable sim-*

ilarities of the death and resurrection of their two Gods. The Pagans argued that their God was older and therefore original. The Christians admitted Christ came later, but claimed Attis was a work of the devil whose similarity to Christ, and the fact he predated Christ, were intended to confuse and mislead men. This was apparently the stock answer— the Christian apologist Tertullian makes the same argument."
(http://home.earthlink.net/~pgwhacker/ChristianOrigins/ PaganChrists_Attis.html, retrieved 12/08/'01)

2. *Adonis of Syria*

   He was born of a virgin mother. He also suffered death for the redemption of mankind, arising from the dead in spring.

3. *Bacchus of Greece or Dionesius*

   He was termed the "only begotten" son of Jupiter. He was born of a virgin named Detemer on December 25th. To his followers, he was "redeemer". He called himself "Alpha and Omega" i.e. similar to the words used for Jesus by the author of the Book of Revelation.

4. *Orisis of the Egyptians*

   He was born of a virgin mother on December 29th. He was betrayed by one Typhen (remember Judas) and was slain. He was buried (just like Jesus), remained in hell for two to three days (just like Jesus), and then rose from the dead (just like Jesus).

5. *Mithra, the Persian Sun-God*

   He was also born of a virgin on the 25th of December. Christmas and Easter were the most important festivals of the Mithras. They also had other surprising similarities with Paul's Christianity like the Eucharist supper etc.

Dr. Arnold Meyer, professor of Theology at the Zurich University, after describing the basic Christian beliefs of today, i.e. the divinity of Christ, atonement etc. states:

> *If this is Christianity, then such Christianity was founded by St. Paul and not by our lord (Jesus or Paul, page 122)*

Source:

Asadi, Muhammed. *Islam or Christianity*. 1989. Karachi, Pakistan

4

WOMEN & RELIGION:

KORAN & THE OPPRESSED WOMAN

We see some common characteristics in modern urban culture concerning what is required of men and women: Open chest shirts for the female, a necktie for the male. Belly exposed shirts for the female, tucked-in shirts for the male. Men's dress patronizes opaque clothing where as feminine clothes are transparent. Modern society labels a man as improperly dressed when not in full suit but women are celebrated if they keep their legs uncovered, even on a cold winter night.

The society that condemns the exhibition of male physical curves and labels them as "perversion" provides artificial aides to under developed areas of the female. Everyone has heard the term, "unwed mother" but you hardly ever hear about the "unwed father" The fashion world usually controlled by males, aims to create instability in the female mind. She is taught that "wearing the least" is something that builds "status" and taking it all off is "liberation".

She is taught to hate her own body. The form of her eyelashes and brows, the style of her walking and speech, the color of her lips, nails and cheek are all given an artificial look. She also hates the natural trend of her hair. In such a society, hair fashion designers, cosmetic manufacturers, and plastic surgeons make big money. Where men balance themselves on a three-inch base heel of the shoes, the woman is expected to balance herself on a half a centimeter heel, creating a medical abnormality. Males make big money, displaying female nakedness through their "respectable" trades like cabarets, strip bars, fashion shows, and especially commercial advertising (Do I want the Mustang or the sexy blonde in the advertisement?), nude paintings magazines and internet web pages.

Modern Western culture does not only show the above but it also shows alarming statistics of single parents, children with no fathers, broken families, sex crimes, divorce, suicide and drug use among teens, asylums for unclaimed children, homes for unwanted parents, clinics for delinquent youth and neurotic adults. Recent estimates suggest that up to 80% of US society displays some form or the other of psychological symptoms, and that up to 22% have psychological problems serious enough to interfere with their day to day living, which are diagnosable (Chicago Tribune 12/1999).

Data in the United States also shows that 25 to 35 percent of girls are sexually abused, usually by men well known to them (Kilbourne 1999:253). A high percentage of women so assaulted suffer from Post Traumatic Stress Disorder (the same disorder that a large number of Vietnam veterans suffer from) that leads to addiction and substance abuse and eventually to poverty and homelessness.

In such societies "liberation" of women has been reduced to a slogan to sell products. Such sellers of "liberation", mostly men, offer women "liberation" via smoking, alcohol, food and their natural longing for stable relationships (which have dwindled in such a society). This commercial "liberation" comes at a great cost to women and serves to isolate them through addiction. As addicts make great consumers, the sellers of such "liberation" want to keep it that way (Kilbourne 1999).

When such sellers of "liberation" are faced with true demands for gender equality, like the ERA (Equal Rights Amendment in the United States), they reject them outright and a government funded and controlled by them makes it fail (ERA failed to pass in 1982). Such powers that be in these societies, not only attack any true efforts towards liberation of women in their own society (as they are commercially disadvantageous to them), but also attack all other ideas presented as truly liberating to women, by other societies (to which they export their commercial culture) by labeling them, "harsh, barbaric, and primitive". They do this through their control of the media, and the support of "pseudo" groups that deliberately distort what they want to deface and misrepresent. The media, if not owned by them, directly depends on them, through their advertising dollars, for its very survival (Kilbourne 1999).

This paper is an attempt to rewrite the history of women's rights and to clarify the position of a book, the Koran on a subject, which has been deliberately distorted and misrepresented through the ages.

WOMEN IN WESTERN RELIGION:

Christianity, the major religion that shaped Western thought, presents women as subordinate to men. Men according to the Bible are the owners of women, just like an animal is owned. Exodus 20:17 which states the famous tenth commandment, lumps a wife together with his servants, animals and house. A man could sell his daughter as a slave (Exodus 21:7-11) or give her in marriage to whomsoever he chose.

This subordination of women to men in the Bible, which shaped Western thought on the issue is made clearer in Leviticus 12:1-8: After the birth of a male child, a woman is ritually impure for seven days, however after the birth of a female child, she is ritually impure for fourteen according to the law of the Bible.

1 Corinthians 14:34-35 of the New Testament of the Bible states:

> *"As in all Churches of the saints, the woman should be subordinate as even the Law says...for it is shameful for a woman to speak in church."*

1 Timothy 2:11 states:

> *"Let a woman learn in silence with all submissiveness. I permit no woman to teach or have authority over men. She is to keep silent,*

for Adam was formed first then Eve, and Adam was not deceived but the woman was deceived and became a transgressor."

1 Corinthians 11:6 says:

"For if a woman will not veil herself then she should cut off her hair, but if it is disgraceful for a woman to be shorn or shaven, let her wear a veil...for man was not created from woman but woman from man. Neither was man created for woman but woman for man."

Jesus' track record, based on the New Testament, isn't much better in his treatment of women, even his own mother. According to the Gospel of John, he is openly rude to his mother. Having become famous among the people, according to John or whoever wrote the Gospel of John, he addresses his mother in this rude manner:

"Woman! What have I to do with you. My time is not yet (John 2:8)."

Imagine, if you're a woman and your son or your daughter said, "Woman! What have I to do with you", how you would feel? Considering a mother's sacrifice and discomfort in bearing and delivering a child, such behavior is unacceptable. Hardly an exemplary character that Christian evangelists depict the "Prince of peace" had. The Koran states:

"Be grateful to God AND the wombs that bore you...(Koran 4:1) "Your mother bore you in discomfort over discomfort..."(Koran 31:14)

The Koran disputes with the idea that the gospels are a genuine account of the words of Jesus, as do the scholars of the Jesus Seminar, based on modern findings. Contrary to what the Gospels present Jesus as saying to his mother, the Koran quotes him as saying:

"And God has made me kind and dutiful towards my mother and not arrogant or overbearing (Koran 19:32)."

Helen Ellerbe, in her book, *The Dark Side of Christian History* (1995) elaborates on the Church's (both Catholic and Protestant) treatment of women:

The second century St. Clement of Alexandria wrote: "Every woman should be filled with shame by the thought that she is a woman." The Church father Tertullian explained why women deserve their status as despised and inferior human beings:

You are the devil's gateway: you are the unsealer of the tree: you are the first deserter of the divine law...You destroyed so easily God's image, man. On account of your desert-that is, death- even the Son of God had to die [Joan Smith, Misogynies: Reflections on Myths and Malice (N.Y Fawcett Columbine, 1989:66)].
Others expressed the view more bluntly. The sixth century Christian philosopher, Boethius, wrote in The Consolation of Philosophy, "Woman is a temple built upon a sewer." Bishops in the sixth century council of Macon voted as to whether women had souls. In the tenth century, Odo of Cluny declared, " To embrace a woman is to embrace a sack of manure..."The Thirteenth Century St. Thomas Aquinas suggested that God had made a mistake in creating woman: "Nothing deficient [or defective] should have been produced in the first establishment of things; so women ought not to have been produced then." And Lutherans at Wittenberg debated whether women were really human beings at all. Orthodox Christians held women responsible for all sin. As the [Roman Catholic] Bible Apocrypha states, "Of woman came the beginning of sin/ And thanks to her we all must die (Ecclesiasticus 25:13-26)."...As 1 Corinthians 7:1 states, "It is a good thing for man to have nothing to do with a woman."

The 1500s marked the beginning of "witchcraft persecutions." By the 1700s over 100,000 people, 80-90 percent of them women, had been put to death in Europe, usually by burning at the stake (Chicago Tribune Dec 29, 1999- A profile of women's history). This amounted to be a self-fulfilling prophecy, as the religious King James I estimated that the ratio of women to men who "succumbed" to witchcraft was twenty to one (Ellerby 1995:116).

Keeping a woman silent according to what St. Paul had said was widely practiced in Europe and the Christian world. In 1833 when the first coeducational college in The U.S, Oberlin College was established, women were not allowed to speak in many classes. In 1623 in England, a woman sentenced by a court to be "too frank" was publicly displayed in a "scold bridle", i.e. a metal cage around her head with a spiked plate which cut her tongue if she dared speak.

Contrary to this God, in the Koran, not only encourages women to speak, but says that they are listened to and admonishes men to be fair and just with them. Consider this statement in the Koran (and compare it to what the Bible said):

> *"God hears the saying of her who argues with you concerning her husband, and complains to God. God hears your mutual complaints…(Koran 57:1)"*

HINDUISM AND WOMEN:

In Hindu religious literature by far, the most effective weapon used by the gods to corrupt virtuous mortals is a woman. Usually a seductive celestial nymph but sometimes, just woman, the root of all evil in the ascetic oriented view of the orthodox Hindu (Baldick, Radice, Jones, page 36).

The Mahabharata states, " I will tell you my son, how Brahma created wanton women and for what purpose, for there is nothing more evil than women… The Lord Grandfather, learning what was in the hearts of the Gods, created wanton women by a magic ritual in order to delude mankind." (13.40.3-10)

The complete subservience of wives to their husbands in Hindu custom shows up in the practice of Sati, where the wife burns herself alive on her dead husbands pyre. In 1780 when the Raja of Marwar died in India, his 64 wives burned themselves alive on his funeral pyre. Even though the secular government of India made this practice illegal, it still continues to be practiced because of religion.

CHINESE RELIGIOUS CONCEPTS AND WOMEN:

The Yin and the Yang is a concept quite familiar even in the west especially in merchandise. In their mythical theory of how the universe operates, Chinese philosophers invented the concept of the Yin and Yang. The universe they concluded is understood to be a balance of the Yin (evil or negative) and the Yang (good or positive).

When asked to further describe Yin (evil), the explanation comes:

> *"The Yin is the negative force in nature. It is seen in darkness, coolness, FEMALENESS, dampness, the earth, moon and the shadows. The Yang (good) is the positive force in nature. It is seen in lightness, warmness, MALENESS, dryness and the sun."* (Hopfe, page 207).

Max Weber, the German sociologist, recognized as a pioneer in sociology and known for his work on the Sociology of Religion, writes in his work on Confucianism and Taoism:

> *The doctrine held in common by ALL schools of philosophy [in Chinese Religion] summarized the "good" spirits as the [heavenly and masculine] Yang principle, the "evil" ones as the [earthly and feminine] Yin principle, explaining the origin of the world from their fusion (Ed. Gerth 1951:29)*

Until 1901, the Chinese practiced "foot binding" for girls, which deformed the girl's feet. It had been practiced for around a thousand years, based on tradition, till it was banned in 1901. Even after being banned, it was widely practiced until 1949. Marie Vento (1998), in her paper, *One Thousand Years of Chinese Footbinding: Its Origins, Popularity and Demise* (retrieved from the Internet 01/15/'00), writes:

> *In its most extreme form, footbinding was the act of wrapping a three- to five-year old girl's feet with binding so as to bend the toes under, break the bones and force the back of the foot together. Its purpose was to produce a tiny foot, the "golden lotus", which was three inches long and thought to be both lovely and alluring...*
> *One notable personality who aided in the spread of footbinding was the famed writer and scholar Zhu Xi (1130-1200 A.D), whose commentaries on the Confucian classics would form the canon of Neo-Confucianism that would dominate Chinese intellectual and philosophical life for six subsequent centuries. An ardent advocate of footbinding, he introduced the practice into southern Fuijan in order to spread Chinese culture and teach proper relations between men and women, greatly influencing other writers who mention the practice as if it were normal...For men footbinding is troubling because it suggests not only that men are capable of perceiving a gruesomely crippled foot as an object of seductive pleasure, but that they are further capable of using their superior social position to coerce women to conform to a standard of beauty that is both deformed and grotesque. For women, footbinding is unsettling because it reveals a willingness to cripple their own daughters to meet an aesthetic and criterion of social behavior defined by men."*

FEMALE INFANTICIDE AND HINDU AND CHINESE TRADITION:

Not only did the Koran outlaw female infanticide, which was widely practiced in Arabia at the time of the prophet Muhammed, it made it an issue to be especially addressed on Judgment Day:

"And when the girl-child buried alive is asked for what sin she was killed…(Koran 81:8-9)"

The Koran places extreme importance on every single human life, be it male or female, of whatever color or nationality. The statement of the Koran reproduced below on the dignity of every single human life is unsurpassed in world literature. The Koran states, without differentiating between male and female:

"…Whosoever kills even one human being, other than man slaughter or tyranny on earth, it would be as if he had killed all of humanity. And whosoever saves even one human life, it will be as if they have saved all of humankind." (Koran 5:32)

Not only is female infanticide widely practiced in India based on the traditional Hindu preference for male children compared to females [resulting in over 10,000 confirmed cases every year- non reported cases are many more], modern technology is being used to abort female fetuses (Naft & Levine 1997:304-307).

Naft and Levine (1997) write in their International Report on the Status of Women:

…Yet since the mid 1970s, when parents found that modern medical techniques could determine the sex of a fetus and enable them to identify and abort female fetuses, the practice has become commonplace…Government officials even suspect that the disproportionate abortion of female fetuses may be a major underlying

cause of the recent decline in the nation's sex ratio (Naft & Levine 1997:304-305)

There is a strong preference among traditional Chinese for boys instead of girls. Until 1992 there was no law in China that outlawed female infanticide. Given the "one child law" and the traditional preference for male children, female infanticide was commonly practiced and resulted in the famous "missing girl" problem (Naft & Levine 1997).

THE KORAN AND WOMEN:

"And among God's signs is this: He created for you mates from amongst yourselves (males as mates for females and vice versa) that you might find tranquillity and peace in them. And he has put love and kindness among you. Herein surely are signs for those who reflect (Koran 30:21)."

Surprisingly egalitarian in its approach, the Koran doesn't agree with men being owners of women like the Bible says, neither does it agree with women being created for or from men like the Bible says nor does it say that women cannot teach nor have authority over men. The Koran also dispels the common myth among other religions in general that a woman is evil by nature and has been created to deceive mankind. The purpose, says that Koran, of mates is that tranquillity and peace emerges through the natural instinct of love and kindness among mates.

People who analyze the Koran however sometimes feel different about many of its verses, which to them suggest that the Koran is in some way putting down women. These verses are a handful and given the nature of this paper, we can go in detail with them.

The verse in the Koran that causes trouble to most liberals and is misused by evangelical Christians is:

> *"Men are the protectors (Qawamoon) of women, because God has given preference to some over others. And because men spend of their property on women. So good women are obedient, guarding even unnoticed that what Allah (God) has asked them to guard. As for those from whom you fear rebellion in this (i.e. guarding their chastity in your absence), i) talk to them, ii) leave them alone in their beds, iii) strike them. If they then obey you, look not for any way against them… (Koran 4:34)."*

The verse in question is quite clear if we don't jump to hasty conclusions. Men have been given the duty to protect and support women. God has given preference to one gender over another in certain duties. Men have been given preference in being the providers of women and women are given preference in caring for a child. Even if divorce separates a man from his wife, he has to seek her help in caring for the child or another female if the mother agrees (Koran 2:233). Men are told to spend of their property on women and not ask the woman for anything, even if she happens to be rich.

Now to the controversial part: The verse asks women to guard even when unnoticed, that which God has asked them to guard. If we have read the Koran carefully, we won't have trouble in determining that God specifically asks women and men to "guard" their chastity (Koran 24:30-31). To the women who cheat on their husbands, the Koran gives a three step, braking mechanism to hasty divorce or worse still capital punishment for adultery.

Step one, the husband should talk to the wife and try to resolve it. Usually, given men's image in popular culture, step one would normally be shouting and cursing and maybe even hitting. Around four million women in the US are severally battered each year. Two to four thousand of them die. Rather unfortunate and avoidable if a braking mechanism exists for people exercising their emotions. Contrary to this, the Koran suggests that talk be the first option.

Step two, the Koran recommends that marital relations be temporarily stopped between the couple, if cheating persists even after a talk.

This would give the woman further opportunity to consider if she'd rather separate from the man and provide for herself after divorce or if she'd rather stay in the current marriage. If however the couple want to separate, which most people would if there was cheating going on, the Koran states in the next verse:

> *"And if you fear a breach between the two (husband and wife), appoint an arbiter from his family and an arbiter from her family. If they (husband and wife) desire amendment, God will make them of one mind. For God is knowing and is aware (Koran4: 35)."*

If however, the woman wants to stay with the man but doesn't quit cheating, i.e. break up the extra marital relationship, then the Koran says resort to Step three, which is implicitly for the woman's own benefit especially in an economically harsh environment. Step three, the Koran says strike them. The word used signifies a single symbolic hit. The word hit in the verse does not represent "beating up" in any way. It is not supposed to injure the woman but is meant to be symbolic. Thus the same word <u>Darab</u>, is used in the Koran to "strike or hit" someone with an example, <u>Darab al masl</u>. If it injures the woman, than the woman according to Islamic law can have the authorities retaliate against the man as he would have broken the law, as for injury there is equal retaliation according to the Koran (5:45).

Here is the situation that warrants step three: the woman doesn't want to end the current marriage and also doesn't want to put an end to her cheating episodes, the Koran suggests that the husband strike her, for her own benefit. This is very liberal. The woman on her own would be under financial hardship and so she wants to use the current marriage relationship. However she also doesn't want to quit cheating on her husband. People, men or women normally aren't so forgiving so as to keep the marriage and accept that the other party remains cheating. Something has to be done to make the relationship compatible, <u>after</u> both talking and temporarily halting marital relationship hasn't worked. However, in all sincerity, I can state confidently that step 3 will never arrive since both the man and the woman are free to end the relationship during the course of step 1 and step 2.

The Koran by making the symbolic hit step 3 is actually controlling human emotions of hitting, which frequently comes before talking and reasoning given popular culture. It makes it virtually impossible that a man going through 1 and 2 will resort to 3 also and not break the marriage before. Where there are difficulties that need to be settled, the Koran provides a very modern and just arbitration system (see Koran 4:35 above). The Koran is concerned to the utmost about women's rights. Human society has usually not given equal opportunity to women, even today in the West. The Koran wants to protect women in a harsh society and at the same time change men's "control-oriented" minds to one that are more reasonable. The method the Koran uses is more result oriented than dogmatic, where both parties are dealt with equitably and with justice.

By making hitting step 3 the Koran effectively controls the anger emotion that is often spontaneous in such situations. Good reasoning and communication, arbitration to settle differences and short suspension of marital relations should effectively do away with any tendency to hit. The Koran is thus not just putting a count of ten between a man and his anger, but days and weeks. It thus gives anger and mistrust a long time and a systematic procedure to get resolved.

Compare the Koran's breaking mechanism for controlling anger to the fact that wife beating was not outlawed in the United States until 1871 [over 13 centuries after the Koran]. Even after being outlawed, in the absence of such procedures contained in the Koran, domestic violence affects at least a third of all women in the United States, over four million annually [this figure is over 80% under represented as most cases go unreported] (Newman 1998). According to the FBI Uniform Crime Report of 1991, it is the leading cause of injury to women 15 to 44. Over a third of women who die in the United States die at the hands of husbands or boyfriends (Kilbourne 1999). I can confidently state that if such a procedure as the Koran presented was internalized not only would women not get injured, there would be more talking and communication and little or no violence at home. The system of the Koran works where just saying, "Don't do it" would not and has not.

This attitude of the Koran to protect women in an economically harsh environment is seen in many places throughout the book. For example, men married to women who then become guilty of lesbianism or bisexuality are told not to throw the women out of their homes but to keep them there till some way is found (Koran 24:3).

The Koran has given some duty preference to men over women and some to women over men. This was mentioned briefly before. However, this doesn't mean that the Koran forbids women from earning their livelihood, if they have no man to support them. Koran 4:22 for example states that for men is what they earn and for women what they earn and that both men and women should seek God's bounty collectively.

PROPERTY LAWS:

Around two hundred years back, women had no property rights in Europe. Islam has given them such since the start. Before the 1840s women had no property rights in America. Property rights in Islam, given the nature of the various relationships that man and women fit under, are surprisingly egalitarian. When a man marries a woman, he has to give a substantial part of his property (according to his means) to the woman as a "marriage gift (_Mahar_)," stated as a man's duty unto God (Koran 4:24).

A woman doesn't have to give anything to a man even if she is rich. It is for this reason primarily that the Koran asks that out of a parents property the son get twice that of the daughter (Koran 4:11). It is expected that the daughter would marry and get a man's property as marriage gift and not have to worry about providing for herself, as it's the man's duty to provide for her. The son on the other hand would

Islamically be expected not only to provide for his potential wife but also give a major part of his property to her as marriage gift.

This however, is not discrimination among the genders. There are specific reasons why the son gets twice that of the daughter. When the conditions are different, the Koran suggests that both male and female get the same amount. For example out of a son's wealth both the father (male) and the mother (female) get equal shares if the deceased had a son.

LEGAL BATTLES:

> *"O believers. When you contract a debt for a given fixed term, record it in writing…and call to witnesses from among your men, two witnesses. And if two men be not present then one man and two women of such as you approve as witnesses, so that if one of them errs, the other admonishes her (Koran 2:82)."*

Both faithful believers and attackers from all camps have abused this particular statement in the Koran. It is presented by them in a generalized form with a concluding statement that Islam considers women's testimony to be half that of men.

The above verse does not talk about testimony in general but only presents one case basically involving financial transactions. It doesn't state any generalization of women's testimony being half that of men, or that two women will equal one man. If interpretation is sought, then a positive one would be that the Koran wants to protect women from being unfairly influenced or pressurized by men. As support for the woman another woman is supplemented, so that if one errs the other reminds her.

The Koran recognizes this difference in men and women, be it social, psychological or biological[1] and adjusts for it to support the woman from being manipulated by men. The end purpose is justice,

---

1. *"and the male is not like the female"* Koran 3:36

which shouldn't offend any reasonable person. In different circumstances however, one woman's testimony is given more weight, where it concerns herself than one man's testimony in the Koran, as it can override it. This case would be when a man (husband) accuses a woman (his wife) of cheating in a relationship but has no witness except his own testimony, which is against her testimony (Koran 24:6-9). The Koran gives women's testimony more weight than a man's!

DRESS:

We read above that the Bible recommends that women veil themselves or shave off their hair. Contrary to what Muslim practice has been for many centuries, the Koran does not ask women to cover themselves from head to toe. Contrary to that it states:

> *"Tell the believing men to lower their gaze and guard their chastity; that is purer for them. And tell the believing women to lower their gaze and guard their chastity, and not to make a display of their beauty except what is apparent, and let them cast a cover over their bosoms.... And turn to Allah (God) altogether, O believers, in order that you might succeed (Koran 24: 30-31)."*

The Koran suggests that *both men and women* dress modestly and guard their chastity. Other than that, the Koran suggests that women put a covering on their chest (bosom) over the regular clothing they wear and not make a wanton display of their beauty (Koran 24:30-31). This does not fit in any way the picture of a woman wearing a *chador* or *burka* [veil] covered from head to toe. It would more closely resemble a picture of a woman wearing a shirt and pants, which do not deliberately reveal her body, with a scarf over her chest (bosom).

Tradition and not the Koran made "tradition based" Muslims bring the veil into Islam from Christian custom (see Paul's saying on the veil). The Koran did not sanction it. The statement in the Koran that talks about dress, talks about both men and women dressing modestly, guarding their chastity and lowering their gaze. It does not discriminate between the sexes except in the case of women it asks them to take an extra covering over their bosoms (chest) only.

POLYGAMY AND THE KORAN:

Two things that come to mind whenever Islam or the Koran is mentioned in the West (in relation to women) are Islamic polygamy and the restrictive Islamic dress for women (the infamous veil). A third thing also commonly crops up when talking about Islam in general and that is terrorism (Jihad or so-called holy war). These three effectively describe the stereotype of Islam held by the West. Like most stereotypes they are based either on ignorance or describe the practice of those that base their actions on tradition other than the Koran. Instead of attacking tradition, those with vested interests attack Islam and the Koran.

There is nothing in Christianity or Judaism against polygamy (polygyny- one man taking more than one wife). Indeed the Old Testament assumes that marriages will be polygamous and laws are constructed based on that assumption. For example, Exodus 21:10 in the Bible states:

> *"If he take to him another wife, her food, her raiment, and her duty of marriage shall he not diminish." (The Bible, Exodus 21:10)*

There is not a word attributed to Jesus in the New Testament, which disallows polygamy. Paul forbade bishops and deacons from marrying more than one wife (1 Timothy 3:2), this implicitly suggests that other were allowed polygamy (polygyny). The insistence on monogamy was an invention introduced by the Roman Catholic Church as late as AD 600 just as the invention of the celibacy of the clergy, the Church being against marriage in general and not only polygamy (Cairncross 1974:70). The early Lutheran Church in Munster, Germany proclaimed polygamy (polygyny) the "ideal form of marriage" (Cairncross 1974:1)

Any mention of polygamy in the West today, among feminists and non-feminists alike evokes feeling of hate. This hate is rooted in Western culture and not religion as we have seen above. The culture that hates polygamy however allows all sexual intercourse between a man and a woman in plurality (as long as it is pre or non-marital). However the same intercourse made "responsible" by marriage in the plural is outlawed and hated.

The Koran severely restricted the open practice of polygamy. There is just one statement in the Koran that deals with polygamy, yet it is misused and inflated by both Muslims and Non-Muslims. It states:

> *"And if you fear that you will not be able to deal justly with the oppressed women [Yatama- literally, the Orphans among women], then marry from among them two or three or four, but if you fear you wont be just [even then], then marry only one (Koran 4:3)."*

The Koran states explicitly above that polygyny is allowed **only** if the women you marry:

1. Belong among oppressed (orphan) women. Men *cannot* pick and choose from "any" women who they want as a second wife.

2. Polygamy is to practiced only if marriage would bring social justice to such women (*"if you fear that you will not be able to deal justly,"* says the Koran), justice that they are otherwise denied.

3. If marrying more than one cannot bring such justice then polygamy is not allowed. Thus the Koran severely restricts and restricted in Arabia, the open practice of polygamy in society.

The Koran does not, like the early Lutheran Church, term polygamy the "ideal" form. According to the Koran, polygamy is a good option only when it brings social justice to the oppressed classes of women.

According to poverty expert William Julius Wilson (1996), 31% of the continually poor in America comprise of "non-elderly" African American women. Now these are among the oppressed classes of women. If polygamy by well established men could bring social justice to them by removing their children and hence future generations from this "cycle of poverty," it is good. It is also recognized by many sociologists and by Dr. Wilson himself that "non-marriage" and the "lack of marriage" is a viable reason in their poverty and status. "Lack or marriage" or a "broken household" is recognized universally by sociologists as contributing to such poverty. It is recognized that divorce and out of wedlock childbearing has resulted in the "feminization of poverty (Schaefer 2000)." In Iraq, after the Gulf War, when thousands of women became widows, restricted polygamy by just individuals would similarly have been very functional.

A country like the United States where the population of women is a few million more than the population of men, especially at older ages, some women can statistically never find husbands if everyone practiced monogamy. Such oppressed women, facing a double jeopardy of sexism and ageism, could be given family life and hence social and economic justice by "restricted" Koranic polygamy, in a male-dominated society.

The Koran is well aware that men misuse polygamy as they are "swayed by the greed of their hearts" (Koran 4:128) and thus puts severe restrictions on the practice of polygamy to protect the rights of women and wives. As a result the only "religious" book that states explicitly, *"...then marry only one* (Koran 4:3)" is the Koran. Monogamy is prescribed for society in general with "restricted" polygamy being allowed when special circumstances warrant it.

DIVORCE:

The Koran by giving women a right to initiate divorce is truly revolutionary. The New Testament, in the supposed words of Jesus, makes divorce an offense similar to adultery, permissible only when the woman has cheated on the husband (Matthew 5:32). The Old Testament states that only a man can initiate divorce (Deuteronomy 24:1).

The Koran, contrary to that states:

> *"...If you both fear that you wont be able to keep within the boundaries of God in marriage, there is no harm if <u>SHE</u> ransom herself..." (Koran 2:229)*

The ransom would of course be the return of the initial property that the man gave her when she got married to him (*the Mahar*).

It is a common misconception that Islam offers a quick divorce. If the man says: "I divorce you," three times to the woman the marriage is nullified, according to popular rumor. This is not true. The Koran offers an elaborate braking system for divorce. A system which is so advanced for its time that it is now being suggested in England to stop careless "quick" divorce, which creates a burden on both the adults and children in question.

The Koran's method of divorce is simple yet very functional. If mind is set on divorce, a divorce statement is written and pronounced in the presence of witnesses (Koran 65:2). Then there is a three month break in which both parties stay together as husband and wife, so that time be given to reconsider (Koran 2:228). After the three-month period, if the man initiated the divorce, he can either take the wife back, if she wants to remain in the marriage, or part. If he takes her back he can initiate divorce only once more in his life with the same woman.

If he takes her back the second time, then he has lost his rights to initiate divorce in the same relationship ever again (Koran 2:229). A woman can buyout her divorce by surrendering the property that was given her by the husband whenever she thinks the marriage wont work out. All through this process, the Koran suggest that help be sought by arbitration (Koran 4:35), one person from the man's side and one from the woman's. Very modern concepts given the history of the Koran.

Yet, the same culture that points fingers at Islam for its "quick" divorce has a divorce rate of over 50 percent. Out of every hundred new marriages in the United States over fifty (old or new), will end in divorce.

Regarding divorce, since the man has been providing for the woman, regardless of who initiated the *divorce* proceedings, the Koran states:

> *"..And for women are <u>rights equal to the rights against them, in what is just</u>. However men have a degree over them (in the context of **divorce** only-read the context) (2:228)."*

It is very clear that this verse is stating that there can be *no absolute equal laws* when conditions on both sides differ. *Giving equal laws under unequal circumstances would be injustice.* The Koran wants equality with justice. Thus women are allowed to divorce a man once (by surrendering the property the man gave her) and the husband can initiate the divorce twice.

Not only is the Koran the only "religious" book that explicitly states, *"and for women are rights equal to the rights against them in justice (2:228)"*, it is more egalitarian than modern laws.

As late as 1982 in the United States for example, the Equal Rights Amendment that called for equal rights for men and women in the law, failed. The Koran truly liberated women over fourteen hundred years back declaring that for women will be rights equal to those against them in justice!

Koran: A Defender of Women's Rights:

> *"And when you men have divorced women, ...then either retain them in kindness if you reconcile, or part with them in kindness.*

Do not retain them to harm them so that you transgress limits. He who does this has wronged himself (Koran 2:231)."
"O believers! It is not lawful for you to inherit women against their will, nor that you should put restrictions on them, that you might take what you had given them...Consort with them in kindness, for if you hate them, it might happen that you hate something in which God has put much good (Koran 4:19)."

While reading the above statements in the Koran take note of the fact that men and women are mentioned together as "equals" in status. This concept is repeated time and again in the Koran based on the common origin of humankind (Koran 4:1). Unlike the Bible, the Koran does not accept the idea that women are created from or for man. As a result, a common notion that is repeated in the Koran is,

"...You (men and women) proceed one from the other (3:195 etc)."

Summary:

Most people may not have any idea on what Islam is or what it stands for but they are all "experts" on the oppressed woman in Islam. After reading the contents of this paper, it should be evident that:

1. Islam is the only religion that gives equal rights to everyone regardless of race or sex. There is no religious book, not even the constitution of the US, which states explicitly like the Koran, *"And for women are rights equal to the rights against them in justice."*

2. The Koran does not ask women to veil themselves completely from head to toe. Such may be Muslim practice in many parts of the world, but it is not sanctioned by the Koran. The Koran merely asks both men and women to dress modestly and not to flout their nakedness. On the other hand, the Bible which many

claim Western civilization was based on, demands that women wear the veil (1 Corinthians11: 6) or risk having their head shaven.

3. Men and women are of equal human status in the Koran (Koran 3:195), however Christian doctrine on which the early American societies were based, had Biblical norms which hold that a woman is subordinate to a man (1 Corinthians 14:34) and are created for man (1 Timothy 2:11)

4. Islam based on the Koran which is very different to the Islam that Muslim masses believe in, gave women the right to property ownership and a voice in legal testimony centuries before such "revolutionary" ideas were even dreamed of by Europeans and their US counterparts.

5. The Koran prescribes polygamy only among the oppressed classes of women, if marriage can better their status in society and is just and equitable. If marriage cannot provide justice to the woman, then the Koran prescribes monogamy as the only option. The only "religious" book going back fourteen centuries, which explicitly states, *"then marry only one (Koran 4:3)",* is the Koran.

6. Within the text of the Koran the ignorant practice of female circumcision, which many people believe is the norm in Islam, is not even mentioned. It is an innovation in Islam, not something that the Koran suggested or prescribed. It is not a part of Islam or the Koran.

7. Islam has never had a problem with women in authority. Even today, Muslim lands have female heads of states. We have yet to see a woman president in the US.

The cure for Sexism and Racism:

> *"O Humankind! We have created you male and female and have divided you into nations and tribes that you recognize each other.*

The best of you in the sight of God is the one most socially aware (<u>Taqwa</u>- literally it means "extremely careful")." Koran 49:13

Division into sexes and nations is merely for the purpose of recognition and has nothing to do with status or one being better than the other according to the Koran.

"And of God's signs is the creation of the heavens and the earth, and the difference in your <u>colors and languages</u>. Indeed in this are signs for those who have knowledge." Koran 30:22

Just like the different languages in the world, the different colors of humankind are a sign of God. They have nothing to do with status of one or the other being better based on language or color.

This chapter does not at all try to defend *Sunni* or *Shia* Islam. The "Islam" believed in by the masses of Muslims (which I refer to as "tradition based" Islam), includes with the Koran other authorities in their "religion". These authorities are *Hadith* [sayings attributed to the prophet] and *fiqh* [so called Islamic jurisprudence]. These sources are not warranted by the Koran and entered Islam centuries after the death of the prophet, in the form that we have today.

They were based on oral traditions unlike the Koran, which was written down from day one. In these "extra-Koranic" sources we find many statements that are derogatory of women and gives them a lower status compared to men. Some statements in the *Hadith* for example compare women to monkeys and dogs and call them bad luck. They even suggest that the woman serve her husband like a "lesser-god". Not only is this outrageous, it goes against the strict monotheism of the Koran. The Koran is the only book of authority in Islam

Bibliography:

1. The Koran: translated from the Arabic.
   References to the Koran, e.g. Koran 24:5 signify, chapter (Sura) 24, Statement (aya) 5.

2. <u>The Bible</u>. Revised Standard Version (1971) and Good News Bible.

3. Hopfe, Lewis M. <u>Religions of the World</u>, fifth edition. Mc Millan Publishing C 1991.

4. Jones, Baldick, Radice<u>. Hindu Myths</u>. The Penguin Classics 1975.

5. Wilson, William Julius. 1996. <u>When Work Disappears</u>. New York

6. Naomi, Neft and Levine, Ann.D. 1997. <u>Where Women Stand: An International Report on the Status of Women in 140 Countries</u>. New York. Random House.

7. Brotman, Barbara. 1000 Years. The Chicago Tribune. December 29, 1999 (Page 1, Section 8).

8. Cairncross, John. 1974. <u>After Polygamy was made a sin</u>. London. Routledge & K.Paul.

9. Ellerby, Helen. 1995. <u>The Dark Side of Christian History</u>. San Rafael. CA. Morningstar Books.

5

MEDIA TERRORISM:

❖

WHAT IS JIHAD?

The media in our society, controlled by people having vested interests, fuels the misinformation and misconception concerning *Jihad*. As a result, a prejudiced attitude is so nurtured that whenever any terrorism takes place, the ones to blame are Muslims. The truth of this statement was demonstrated in the Oklahoma City Bombing incident of late April 1995. The damage so done by such cowardly acts of literary terrorism by the media, surpass national boundaries and create a culture of hate.

This chapter is divided into three sections: i) Jihad and Islamic warfare, ii) Islam in history and iii) Peace in Islam

I) Jihad and Islamic Warfare:

The word *Jihad* translated into English does not mean "Holy War" as people in the media ignorantly state. In the text of the whole Koran, the word "Holy War" cannot be found. The word Jihad in Arabic means, "struggle".

Jihad as the Koran makes clear, is struggle in the way of God with oneself, and one's possessions. Islam only allows war as a defense. In the case of war, the attack is only to be directed against those who are fighting you. If the enemy kills your civilians even then you are not supposed to kill their civilians till you are sure that those "civilians" are fighting against you to similarly kill you.

> *"Fight in the way of God against those who fight against you, but begin not hostilities. Indeed God does not love transgressors (Koran 2:192-193)."*

If the people you are fighting ask for peace, the Koran states that Muslims have an obligation to accept the peace and fight no more:

> *"..So if they hold aloof from you and wage not war against you and offer you peace. God allows you no way against them (Koran 4:90)."*

The Koran is very lenient even towards prisoners of war (i.e. those who are fighting against you who get captured):

> *"And if any of the idolaters seeks of you protection, grant him (her) protection till he hears the words of God, then convey him to his place of security. That is because they are a folk who know not..(Koran 9:6-8)."*

The Koran states that sometimes war is a necessity and has to be fought to check tyranny:

> *"How is it with you that you do not fight in God's way, when the feeble among the men, women and children are saying, "Our lord, bring us forth from this place whose people are tyrants. O God give us from your presence some protector and helper.'(Koran 4:75-76)."*

> *"..If God had not repelled some people by means of others, the earth would have been corrupted (Koran 2:251)."*

Sometimes, war is a necessity, for the cause of justice and to remove oppression, and as such it is very good and noble:

"Warfare is ordained for you though it is hateful for you. Yet it may happen that you will hate a thing even though it is good for you and love a thing that is bad for you. God knows, you don't know (Koran 2:216)."

ii) Islam in History

The West has generally nourished the idea that Islam spread at the point of the sword. This reasoning led to the prejudice of Islam and terrorism taking root in Western society throughout Europe and America because of the acts of a few misled, ill informed, uneducated people who called themselves "Muslims". This idea nurtured deliberately by the elite in the West and fictitiously imposed upon Islam was adopted by segments of the Islamic world that are easily misled because of a lack of education. The label applied by the West to Islam, thus became a self-fulfilling prophecy among such groups. It is important to note here that "Muslim" and "Islam" is not a label. It signifies states of affairs, a complete submission to God's will as contained in the Koran. The Koran condemns all forms of terrorism and war directed against civilians and non-aggressors.

The Koran is explicit on the freedom of conscience:

"There is no compulsion in religion. Truth is clear from falsehood (Koran 2:256)

"You are in no way a tyrant or forcer over them; but warn by the Koran him who fears my threat (Koran 50:45)."

History gives a lie to the "fairy tale" that Islam spread by the sword:

- Muslims ruled over Spain for 736 years. If the Muslims had used any force during those 736 years to convert the Christians to Islam there wouldn't have been a single Christian left to kick out the Muslims after 736 years of rule.

- Over 150 million Muslims live in Indonesia, yet no Muslim army ever invaded any of its over 2000 islands. Similar is the case with Malaysia, and the east coast of Africa. Odd instances of "Muslims" not guided by the Koran, forcing people to accept their "Islam" may be found. Similar cases can be found in Christianity or with any other religions group.

> *"Charlemagne's conversion of the saxons to Christianity was not by preaching." (THOMAS CARLYLE, ON HEROES AND HERO WORSHIP, 1918: 80)*

Theory and action need to be separated for the purpose of pure research. Islam should be judged based on its "system doctrine" found only in the Koran and not "Muslim" action. Bad "Muslims" don't condemn Islam, just like bad Christians don't condemn Christianity. Hitler was a self proclaimed Christian. Do his acts condemn Christianity?

> *"My feelings as a Christian points me to my Lord and Savior as a fighter. It points me to the man who once in loneliness, surrounded by a few followers, recognized these Jews for what they were and summoned men to fight against them and who, God's truth! was greatest not as a sufferer but as a fighter. In boundless love as a Christian and as a man I read through the passage which tells us how the Lord at last rose in His might and seized the scourge to drive out of the Temple the brood of vipers and adders. How terrific was His fight for the world against the Jewish poison. Today, after two thousand years, with deepest emotion I recognize more profoundly than ever before the fact that it was for this that He had to shed His blood upon the Cross. As a Christian I have no duty to allow myself to be cheated, but I have the duty to be a fighter for truth and justice... And if there is anything which could demonstrate that we are acting rightly it is the distress that daily grows. For as a Christian I have also a duty to my own peo-*

ple. -Adolf Hitler, in a speech on 12 April 1922 (Norman H. Baynes, Ed. The Speeches of Adolf Hitler, April 1922-August 1939, Vol. 1 of 2, pp. 19-20, Oxford University Press, 1942)

History is clear:

> *"History makes it clear however that the legend of fanatical Muslims sweeping through the world and forcing Islam at the point of the sword upon conquered races is one of the most fantastically absurd myths that historians ever repeated." (DE LACY O`LEARY, ISLAM AT THE CROSS ROADS, LONDON 1923)*
> *"The greatest success of Muhammad's life was effected by sheer moral force without the stroke of a sword." (EDWARD GIBBON, HISTORY OF THE SARACEAN EMPIRE, LONDON 1817)*

iii) Peace and Islam

The word Islam comes from the Arabic root word *Salaam*, which means peace. The universal greeting of Muslims is *"As Salaam o Aleykum"*. It means: "peace be with you." The Koran, the only book of authority on Islam encourages peace making among humankind.

The idea of a "United Nations" working for world peace is actually borrowed from the Koran:

> *"There is no good in much of their secret conferences except, him who enjoins alms giving and kindness and <u>peace making</u> among mankind. Whoever does that seeking the good pleasure of God? God will bestow on him (her) a vast reward (Koran 4:114)."*

Islam gives a worldview of a close relationship between all men & women based on a common essence of creation [Koran 4:1] and only one creator God.

"O Humankind! We have created you males and females, and have divided you into nations and tribes so that you may recognize each other. The best among you in the sight of God is the one most careful [of the truth] (Koran 49:13)."

Source:

Asadi, Muhammed. Jihad & Warfare (**http://www.geocities.com/ rationalreality/jihad.htm**)

6

SCIENTIFIC REVELATION:

KORAN & CRITICAL RATIONALISM

> "Say: What thing is greatest in testimony? Say: God is witness between you and I, and that this Koran has been inspired in me that I many warn with it you and whomsoever it be conveyed to…" (Koran 6:19)

Religion throughout the history of humankind has had a tremendous hold on humanity. According to Emile Durkheim, the French Sociologist, the first organized institutions of mankind were religious in character. Even today religion is of primary importance to millions of individuals who try to live by it and give it a special place in their lives. Therefore any issue involving religion in today's world is worthy of discussion. Science, in its popular usage, is generally defined as the systematic observation of natural phenomena and their workings. Since the industrial revolution in the eighteenth century it is seen as the thing in control of human destiny and its future. Those who fail to apply it to their lives are kept at the lowest strata of society in today's highly competitive world. As today, both science and religion are widespread, each having dogmatic believers, antagonism has resulted. The common notion being that science and religion are opposites; i.e. they repel each other as like poles of a magnet.

According to the sociologist Max Weber, in his article, *Science as a Vocation,* science has resulted in the "disenchantment" of the world. The "enchantment" of the world was due to, according to him, people relying on religion and giving magical explanations to perfectly logical, natural phenomena.

This article attempts to use the Koran to examine Max Weber's claims about religion. The source of Islam is a book, just one book, the Koran. Modern Islam however has added other sources, which the Koran doesn't validate. The Koran, is historically the earliest written text we possess in the the Arabic language and as such is the only valid authority on Islam as conveyed by the prophet Muhammed. The other sources *Hadith* and *Fiqh* date from over 200 years after Muhammed's death. I will therefore not deal with these other sources as they do not represent the "original" Islam, so to speak.

Within its text, the Koran names itself many times as a book revealed directly by God, in which God is speaking in the first person. The Koran, is historically the only book of authority on Islam and the earliest written text available in the Arabic language, says that true believers, *"reason about the origin of the heavens and the earth (Koran 3:190-191)."* This itself is science by definition when done in a systematic way. By doing that a person gets to the truth by discovering the "nature of God" [His *Sunna-* in Arabic], as reflected by his creation and confirmed by His revelation the Koran. The contrary to the concept of a "supernatural", the Koran talks about nature and creation being an expression of God's attributes. We can look inside the *"Mind of God"* so to speak by studying his creation.

Arthur J Arberry, in the introduction to his translation of the Koran states, *"The Koran is a book apart.."* The Koran, in its contents and presentation is indeed a book apart. The amazing thing about the Koran, given the time of its origin is that it does not contain any scientific inaccuracies or errors. Such errors would have been unavoidable if the Koran had a human origin. Not only that, the Koran preempted many of today's hard earned scientific facts, which just a hundred years back would have been impossible to discover. We possess written documents of the Koran going back at least fourteen centuries.

The scientific system of inquiry is emphasized time and again by the Koran. The linking of science and rationality with the verses of the Koran is not only legitimized but also encouraged by God in the Koran. The Koran tells the reader that if he/she does not know something or are unsure that they should ask "those who are informed" (people having information, 25:59). In the case of all the scientific and natural phenomena discussed in the Koran, the people having knowledge and information would most definitely be the scientists. Thus the Koran discourages unreasoned belief.

A critical and scientific analysis of the Koran is encouraged by the Koran in this statement:

> *"Do they not carefully consider the Koran. If it had been from anyone other than God, they would have found in it many contradictions."*

If the Koran is indeed the word of the Creator, then it must be error-free when it discusses details about proven facts of science, like description of stages in embryology. For example, the details about embryology in the Koran are presented in a fashion that would facilitate belief only after those verses have been checked by known findings. They are presented as a challenge:

> *"If you are in doubt then (consider this).... (22:5 etc)"*

The same is also witnessed throughout the Koran when the book makes statements like, *"Do you not know.... (Or) Have you not seen and considered, etc."* Also consider all the falsification tests contained in the Koran, like the one which challenges people to produce a chapter comparable to the Book. All these legitimize and encourage a rational/scientific inquiry into the truthfulness of the Koran.

Maurice Bucaille, who was one of the first to popularize the linking of the Koran and Science, in his best selling books, *The Bible, the*

Quran and Science, and *What is the Origin of Man?*, showed that given the history of the origin of the Koran, it could not have been the work of a man or group of men living in Arabia or anywhere else at that time. Lecturing at the French Academy of Medicine, he concluded on the subject:

> *"It makes us deem it quite unthinkable for a man of Muhammed's time to have been the author of such statements on account of the state of knowledge in his day. Such considerations are what give the Koranic revelation its unique place and forces the impartial scientist to admit his inability to provide an explanation which calls solely on materialistic reasoning."(Bucaille 1985)*

Keith L. Moore, head of the department of anatomy, at the University of Toronto, was shown verses of the Koran dealing with the microscopic stages of the human embryo. He was so surprised at what he found that he went back and revised the history of embryology in his standard texts on the subject. The books that Keith L. Moore authored are taught at prestigious institutions like Yale and all around the world. He stated concerning the issue:

> *"It is clear to me that these statements (in the Koran on embryology) must have come to Muhammad from God. This proves to me that Muhammed must have been the messenger of God or Allah." (Rehaili 1995)*

Professor Marshall Johnson, surprised at what the Koran had to say on geology, sates:

> *" There is nothing here in conflict with the concept that divine intervention was involved in what he (Muhammed) was able to say." (Rehaili 1995)*

Consider yourself an inhabitant of 7th Century Arabia. Society has very little scientific knowledge. Myth and magic control people's thoughts. How far would you go if you wanted to discover the true origin or the universe? How much progress would you make if you wanted to uncover the origin of life? We can move away from Arabia and scan the world scene at that period in history. Nothing in the literature of the world comes even remotely close to the accuracy of statements about the natural world contained in the Koran. In fact some of the information that we come across in the Koran wasn't known till about 40 years back and some of it wasn't known until the day it was read in the Koran by scientists just a few years ago.

Bertrand Russell the famous English philosopher and celebrated agnostic in his book, *Religion and Science*, states, "*I cannot admit any method of arriving at the truth except that of science*" (page, 18). That is the method that I use throughout this study, and the end conclusion is an arrival at truth, that which in the words of Jesus is liberating.

The Koran claims to originate with the one (God) who originated everything (Koran 55:2). Therefore, we have every right to logically inquire if the originator of the earth and the heavens, in the knowledge that he gives us about them knows what we have discovered about their origin through modern science.

The Koran exists in the world today. Therefore, if we do not accept the book's claim of being a revelation, then we must come up with an explanation as to its origin. The existence of the Koran cannot be denied; we have a problem, which demands an explanation to justify denial, if denial were our choice.

People who reject the Koran's claim throughout the ages have come up with explanations and theories as to the origin of the Koran. No matter what the details of the particular theory might be, they all reduce to basically two hypotheses:

> i) ammad was a liar. He got his information from the outside and presented it to people as a revelation from God. The proponents of this hypothesis claim that Muhammad who "borrowed" information from other sources, composed the Koran. Some even suggest

that Muhammad was helped by a "group" of people to compose the Koran.

ii) second hypothesis suggests that Muhammed was deceived or deluded in that he believed that he was a prophet when in fact he was not. To the people who offer this hypothesis, the Koran is the product of the "deluded" mind of Muhammed. Muhammad's hallucinations.

It may sound surprising but the book that is being attacked, the Koran, is also well aware of these two hypothesis that people have been presenting throughout the ages in trying to reject it:

Hypothesis 1 suggests that Muhammad was a liar. The Koran states:

"They (the rejecters) say: 'These are tales of the ancients, which he has caused to be written down so that they are dictated to him morning and evening (Koran 5:25)."

Hypothesis 2 suggests that Muhammed was self-deceived. The Koran states:

"The ones who reject almost trip you up by glaring at you when they hear The Reminder (Koran), and they say,' He is indeed deranged (Koran 68:51)."

Most people who present these in the form of theories, are forced to take them together in conjunction. Logically speaking however, both these hypothesis are mutually exclusive and cannot be taken together. They can stand on their own, if facts support them, but taken together they collapse. As an example: If a man is a liar (Hypothesis 1) then when someone asks the man a question, he has to search for the answer. He looks either within himself for the answer or asks his friends in secrecy so that he can give the inquirer a satisfactory response. He knows that he is not a prophet so he has to lie to convince the questioner. On the other hand, if the man is deluded (Hypothesis

2) then when someone asks the man a question, he does not search for the answer, if he doesn't know it. He is deluded, self-deceived, he believes he is a prophet and the answer will be given to him by revelation. A large section of the Koran came as answers to questions that people would ask.

To repeat the above, if the man is a liar, he knows he is not a prophet and investigation can provide evidence as to where the material came from but if he is deluded, even though the material presented is his own hallucinations, still he cannot be termed a liar for he believes he is a prophet. If a man is a liar then he is not self-deceived, if he is self-deceived then he is not a liar. Therefore Hypothesis 1 and Hypothesis 2 cannot be mixed up in explaining the Koran. However, what we see is that people need both excuses to explain certain things in the Koran. They often start by presenting Hypothesis 1 (Muhammed was a liar) and end up with Hypothesis 2 (Muhammed was self-deceived), i.e. Muhammed was a liar and self-deceived. This cannot be, logically speaking as we have seen above.

It may again surprise you but the Koran is also aware of this illogical stand that people take by terming Muhammad both a liar and self deluded. The Koran states:

> *"And they have turned away and said, 'One taught (by others), and a madman (44:14)."*

The Koran can be Hypothesis 1) The product of a liar, or Hypothesis 2) The product of a deceived mind, or it can be what it claims to be, i.e. God's revelation; **_but_** it can never be both Hypothesis 1 and Hypothesis 2 at the same time.

> *"And We certainly know that there are those among you who reject it (the Koran). But it is indeed a sorrow for the rejecters, for it is indeed the certain truth (Koran 69:49-51)."*

Hypothesis 1 and its implications:

If the Koran is the product of a man's mind who is a "liar", who got his information from the outside and then presented it to the world as a revelation then:

1. We have to explain the *confidence* portrayed by the various statements in the Koran. A confidence that shows that whosoever is presenting this is convinced that he indeed has the truth. As examples:

—The Koran challenges people to find a mistake in the book (chapter 4, verse 82). Now only a person who is convinced about what he has can make such a claim. Do you know of any book that makes a claim that it is 100% error free? The Bible never makes such a claim.

—Another example would be the invitation given to Christians who dispute with Muslims about the nature of Jesus as presented in the Koran. The verse says:

"Come let us call our sons and your sons…our families and your families and let us ask God to curse the ones who are lying (about the true information on Jesus) (Koran 3:61)."

This shows that whoever is presenting this is confident and sure that he has the truth on which the challenge is based.

—Another example of this *confidence* that a liar is incapable of portraying, is the account of when the Meccans, who wanted to kill Muhammad, came unto the mouth of the cave in which he and his friend Abu-Bakr were hiding. Abu-Bakr was afraid, Muhammed told him to "relax", "God will save us," he told him. Now if the man is a liar, one who lies to convince people that he is a prophet, you might expect him to say, "Go and look for a back way out," or "lie low and be quiet." But what he actually said shows that he had no doubt that he was a prophet and that God would save them. Hypothesis 1 cannot explain the above in the Koran.

2. If the Koran is a lie, the product of a man's lying mind, how do you account for:

The Koran claims that it contains information that was "new" to the people it was being read to. The Meccans hated Muhammad, if this statement in the Koran was not true and the information was not "new" they would have loved to point out the source. Yet they never answered this challenge to produce similar "knowledge" as the Koran (chapter 46: verse 4)

As proof of the above, I'll give two examples:

1. The Koran mentions the wall of "Zulqarnain," the two-horned one. It gives a complete description of this wall and how it was built to protect a people from outside invaders (Koran 18:96-98). The Arabs had never heard of it, or what it looked like, neither had the Arab Jews or the Arab Christians. Now, after the death of the prophet, they were curious about this wall mentioned in the Koran. Omar the Khalif sent out travelers to verify the existence of this wall. It is in Durbent in the former Soviet Union. It is referred to as Alexander's wall however modern historians dispute on whether Alexander had anything to do with it.

Compare what the Koran said over fourteen centuries back, before any Arab had set foot on Derbent to what the Columbia Encyclopaedia says:

"Derbent was founded (A.D 438) by the Persians as a strategic fortress at the Iron Gates. There are remains of the Caucasian Wall (also called Alexander's Wall), built by the Persians in the 6th century. as a bulwark against northern invaders. (6th Edition, 2000)."

If Muhammed was a liar, who told him about this wall thousands of miles to the east, about which no one in his area knew anything?

2. The Koran mentions a city by the name of Iram where a prosperous people the AAD lived. It was a city of "tall pillars":

"Have you seen how your sustainer (God) dealt with the Aad people? Iram, of the lofty pillars (Koran 89:8-8)"

Until very recently no historic or non-historic record existed about Iram. However in 1973, the ancient city of Ebla was excavated in Syria. While going through the tablet library of Ebla archaeologists came across a list of cities that Ebla traded with and on that list was a city named Iram. When reporting it in the National Geographic of December 1978, the only reference to Iram they could cite other than the tablets was the Koran, chapter 89.

In 1992 using SIR-C imaging [Synthetic Aperture Radar] using the Space Shuttle, GPR [Ground Penetrating Radar] and GMT [Geophysical Diffraction Tomography], scientists discovered Iram [also called Ubar] in southern Oman, buried under 12 meters of sand. The city contained evidence of "tall pillars" exactly as mentioned in the Koran chapter 89. The Koran described this fact; over fourteen centuries back at a time when no one in the world could have had access to this city.

Now, if Muhammad was a liar where did he get his information? He had no way of knowing the above, since all the legends about *Iram* postdate the Koran.

Hypothesis 2 and its implications:

Hypothesis 2, suggests that the Koran is the product of a man's deluded mind. If the Koran is a product of a man's hallucinations then what comes out as a result are things that are in his mind. What do you think went on in Muhammed's mind? He didn't have an easy life. He was an orphan to start with, then his grandfather who looked after him died, then his uncle who adopted him. After that, his life companion, his wife died. All his children except for one daughter died in his lifetime. Does the Koran reflect any of this? It doesn't even mention these things at all. Yet these were the things that surely bothered him and caused him pain through his whole life, but they never show up in a book, which is said to be the product of his deluded mind!

In fact, the information contained in the Koran is such that no man living anywhere in that day or age could have known. I'll give a few examples, which should make the point clear:

1. The Origin of Life:

The Koran mentions that all life *originated* from water (Koran chapter 21, verse 30) and that man himself is "created" of water and so are all the animals on earth (Koran 25:54, and 24:45). Now these statements to an Arab would have sounded atrocious in that day and age. Even today such statements in the Koran might cause you to wonder if scientific facts about them are unknown. The fact that all life originated in water is well established by the scientific community today. They have evidence to support the fact that the first living beings were algae, and they existed in water. The fact that human beings and animals are created of water is also well established since cytoplasm the basic component of "life" in any animal cell is over 80% water.

2. Maturity:

The Koran mentions that a human being reaches full maturity at age forty (Koran 46:15). This is a very unusual statement. Even today most people believe that full maturity is reached at puberty and laws usually put it between 18-21. However, the Koran is scientifically correct where even modern ideas are wrong. If we analyze the statement psychologically and physiologically, what we find is that the "overall quantity of stored knowledge in the mind of an individual reaches a peak at age thirty-nine and after that it gradually declines." Arthur C. Guyton, in his standard textbook on physiology, *Physiology of the Human Body* (6th Ed), which is the standard textbook in many medical schools around the world, states this on page 207.

3. The Female Bee:

The Koran mentions the bee, which leaves its home in search for food, in the verses that discusses honey (Koran 16:68, 69). It uses the female verb in describing the bee, in Arabic *faslukee*. This, to the Arab, suggests that the bee, which leaves its home in search for food, is female.

Does anyone except an expert know how to differentiate between a male and a female bee? Even today, let alone Muhammad's time, 1400 plus years back, we need a specialist to differentiate between a male and a female bee. The Koran is accurate when it mentions that the female bee leaves its home in search of food; the males never leave their homes for food, it is the females who have to feed them.

4. Embryo Sex Determination:

The Koran says that the "ejaculated drop" determines the sex of a human baby (Koran 53:45). It is common knowledge that semen is the fluid that is ejaculated by males during sexual acts. Females do not possess such "ejaculated semen."

The sex of the baby, whether it be male or female, will indeed be determined by the 'ejaculated drop', i.e. the father's sperm, as mentioned by the Koran. It has been scientifically established only recently that the female ovum contains only X-chromosomes. If the ejaculated drop, the father's sperm bears the Y chromosome, the offspring will be male, otherwise the offspring will be female. No one living at the time of Muhammed or even Darwin for that matter had any knowledge of such genetics foretold centuries earlier in the Koran.

5. The Invisible Barrier:

The Koran states that there are two seas that meet but don't intermingle because of a barrier between them (Koran 55:19-20). It is a necessity that seas intermingle through straits between them. The Koran however is aware of a very unusual phenomenon, which scientists discovered only recently. The Mediterranean and Atlantic oceans differ in their chemical and biological constitution. The French scientist Jacques Yves Cousteau conducted various undersea investigations at the Strait of Gibraltar and explaining these phenomena concluded:

> "Unexpected fresh water springs issue from the southern and northern coasts of Gibraltar. These mammoth springs gush towards each other at angles of 45 degrees forming a reciprocal dam. Due to this fact the Mediterranean and the Atlantic Oceans cannot intermingle (as quoted by Nurbaki)."

Did Muhammed do research on the chemical and biological components of seawater to discover this unusual phenomena?

6. The Gaseous Universe:

The Koran mentions that the universe, at a point in its origin was a "gaseous material." (Koran 41:11). It uses the Arabic word *Dukhan*, which stands for smoke. A perfect analogy for gas and particles in suspension and the gasses being hot.

Scientists have only very recently confirmed that the universe did indeed originate from a gaseous mass composed of hydrogen and helium, a big mass of hot gasses, a mass over 300,000 times that of the earth. That mass then fragmented to form galaxies. Muhammad, who had no formal schooling of any kind, could not have possibly known this.

7. The Big Bang:

The Koran gives an accurate visual description of the Big Bang theory of the creation of the universe. The Koran states:

> "Do not the rejecters see that the heavens and earth were a unit joined together then we split them apart" (Koran 21:30).

This is exactly how the 'rejecter' scientists envision the creation of the universe, from one singularity, which then exploded, termed the 'big bang'. The Koran told us about the "common origin" of everything in the universe much before scientists described it in the 20th century. How do we explain this information in the Koran if it is not what it claims to be, the words of an all-knowing creator?

Professor Alfred Kroner, chairman of the Department of Geology at the Institute of Geosciences, Johannes Gutenburg University, Mainz, Germany stated about this verse in the Koran:

> *"Somebody who did not know something about nuclear physics 1400 years ago could not, I think, be in a position to find out from his own mind for instance that the earth and the heavens had the same origin, or many others of the questions that we have discussed here."(Rehaili 1995)*

8. The Expanding Universe:

The Koran talks about a universe that is continually "expanding" (Koran 51:47). The concept of an expanding universe is very popular with scientists today, however no one knew of it until recently. Do you know that the universe is expanding? Can you feel or see it expanding? No, the verification of this requires specialized knowledge and instruments, which no one at the time of Muhammad had, access to. The Koran states:

> *"And the sky we built it with might and We cause the 'expansion' of it (Koran 51:47)."*

9. The Death of Stars:

The Koran mentions the 'death of stars' (Koran 77:7-8). Astronomers including Dr. Patterson of Southwest Missouri State are surprised at finding this information in the Koran. They know that at the time of Muhammad, people believed that once a thing was formed, it was permanent. The Koran is very accurate when it mentions dying stars. Our own sun is a dying star.

10. The Phases of the Moon:

The Koran talks about the phases of the moon (36:38-39). There is no book, to my knowledge, that predates the Koran that mentions the modern term "phase" in connection with the moon. Dr. Patterson confirms this. The Arabic word used for "phase" in the Koran is <u>Manazil</u>.

11. The Movement of the Sun:

The Koran mentions the movement of the sun. The sun's movement is not something that is evident to our eyes or experience but requires specialized equipment. The Koran states in chapter 36, verse 39:

> *"And the sun constantly journeys towards a homing place for it and for the moon, We have determined phases (36:39)."*

Modern science has found out that the sun rotates around its axis every 26 days (signified in the Koran by the verb *Yasbahoon*) and is continually on a journey in space towards its homing place the *solar apex*, just like mentioned in the Koran 36:39. How could Muhammed have known these facts if the Koran is the product of his delusional or lying mind?

12. The Roots of Mountains:

The Koran states that mountains are like "tent-pegs", i.e. they have a root extending down into the earth like "anchors" and this gives stability and balance to the earth.

> *"Have we not expanded the earth and made the mountains as tent pegs" (Koran 78:6-7)*

> *"We have cast into the earth anchors lest it shake with you" (Koran 31:10 etc.)*

This fact was discovered less than 150 years ago by scientists and now accepted as a fundamental law in geology, the concept of isostacy. M. J Selby in a standard-text on the subject entitled *"Earth's Changing Surface* (Clarendon Press, Oxford 1985) states:

> *"G.B Airy in 1855 suggested that the crust of the earth could be likened to rafts of timber floating on water. Thick pieces of timber float higher above the water surface than thin pieces and similarly thick sections of the earth's crust will float on a liquid or plastic substratum of greater density. Airy was suggesting that mountains have a deep root of lower density rock, which the plains lack. Four years after Airy published his work, J.H Pratt offered an alternative hypothesis…By this hypothesis, rock columns below mountains must have a lower density, because of their greater length, than shorter rock columns beneath plains. Both Airy and Pratt's hypothesis imply that surface irregularities are balanced by differences in density of rocks below the major features (mountains and plains) of the crust. This state of BALANCE is described as the concept of ISOSTACY (Selby1985:32) ."*

13. Microscopic Embryology:

The Koran is known to be the first book to give microscopic details of human embryology, hundreds of years before the discovery of the microscope! The Koran contains information on embryology, which was not discovered till about 30 years back and certain details were new even to modern scientists but were immediately confirmed as being accurate.

The Koran mentions that at a certain stage, the developing human is like "*allaqa*", a leech-like clot. If you take a microscopic picture of a human embryo of days 7-12 and place it next to a picture of a leech, they both look identical. Not only do they look the same but they function in the same way too. Just like a leech derives nourishment from its host's blood, the embryo derives nourishment from the decidua or the pregnant endometrium. These facts about the Koran are well documented and listed by Keith L. Moore in his standard textbooks on embryology, books used in medical schools all across the world.

14. Koran on Nerve Endings:

> "*Indeed, those who disbelieve in our signs, we will roast them at a fire. As often as their skins are wholly burned, we will give them in exchange other skins, that they may taste the punishment (Koran 4:56).*"

It is well known to specialists today that full thickness burns destroy nerve endings, so that further burning a person after that wont cause any pain. In Bailey and Love's *,Short Practice of Surgery* (20th edition), it states:

> "*...Full thickness burns are relatively painless due to the destruction of nerve endings..*" (page, 149)

In order to determine full or partial thickness loss, doctors use the "pin prick" test. How such information could have been known at the time of Muhammed is baffling to people who would attribute a human origin to the Koran. The Koran states clearly that people will be given a "new skin" for the purpose of pain, thereby linking skin loss with the loss of nerve endings, which cause pain.

15. Resurrection of the Dead:

> "*What, does humankind think that they will be left to roam at will? Was he not a drop ejaculated? Then he was a leech-like structure. And He (God) created and formed. And made of him a pair, the male and the female. What, is He (God) then not able to quicken the dead?*" Koran 65:36-40

The above verse of the Koran questions those who reject the notion of the resurrection of the dead. What is the more difficult task: That you were created from an insignificant drop, which was so small that it couldn't be seen except through a microscope, or that one day you will be formed from your remnants?

> "What, does man think that We shall not put his bones together again? Yes indeed, We are able to shape his very fingers (Koran 75:3-4)."

Russian scientists recently discussed reproducing an extinct species of elephant by use of a microscopic unit of long-dead gene material. No one in the scientific community said that that was unreasonable. The point is that the resurrection of the dead might be an unusual think but it certainly is not unreasonable. The use of cloning techniques throws further light on the amazing nature of the Koranic verse which compares the resurrection of the dead with human development from an insignificant zygote to the fetus. Cloning provides theoretic and empirical evidence for the resurrection of the dead.

16. The Circulation of Blood:

> "And surely in the cattle, there is a lesson for you. We give you to drink of what is inside their bodies, from between digested food and blood, pure milk, pleasant to those who drink it (Koran 16:6)."

The above verse of the Koran calls our attention to the food distribution function of blood. It should be kept in mind however that a Muslim scientist formally discovered the circulation of blood 600 years after Muhammed's death and it was made known to the West by William Harvey, 1000 years after Muhammed had died. If Muhammed was the author of the Koran how would he have known, at the time that he lived that digested food is transported via blood and then becomes the constituent of milk secreted by the mammary glands?

17. The "Constants":

"Do they [the disbelievers] not see that God has subjected for them whatsoever is in the heavens and on earth (Koran 31:20)?
"Indeed We have calculated for everything a set measure."(Koran)
"The Most Merciful (God), uplifted the sky and set the balance."
(Koran 55:7)

Compare these statements in the Koran to what the physicist Paul Davies writes in his book, *The Accidental Universe* (1982):

"The numerical values that nature has assigned to the fundamental constants, such as the charge on the electron, the mass of the proton, and the Newtonian Gravitational constant, may be mysterious, but they are critically relevant to the structure of the universe that we perceive. As more and more physical systems from nuclei to galaxies have become better understood, scientists have begun to realize that many characteristics of these systems are remarkably sensitive to the precise value of the fundamental constants. Had nature opted for a slightly different set of numbers, the world would have been a very different place and we would not be here to see it." (Davies 1982)

At around 300,000 years after the big bang, all parts of the universe, even separated by more than 20 times the horizon distance, and expanding in opposite directions, in causally disconnected regions (i.e.. no cause or physical effect could pass from one region to the other), began to expand with the same expansion rate and temperature.

No natural explanation exists to explain how a chaotic explosion, the big bang resulted in a uniform expansion pattern among causally disconnected regions, expanding in opposite directions. Calculations indicate that when the universe was a trillionth of a trillionth of a trillionth second old, it consisted of 10 to the power 80 <u>causally disconnected</u> regions, and no physical effect could have traveled from one region to another and yet 300,000 years after, cosmic background radiation proves that they all started expanding with the same expansion rate and the same temperature. It was as if they acted upon uniformly communicated intelligent direction. The "Inflation" explanation implies the same. Consider what the Koran says:

> "... And He (God) inspired in all the heavens their mandate (Koran 41:12)."

The "Flatness" or "smoothness" of the universe is established by modern science and leads scientists to wonder as to how a uniform distribution of matter resulted from the big bang. The Koran is aware of this and presents the "smoothness" of the universe as a challenge to unbelievers:

> "[It is God] who has created the multiple skies, one separate from the other (as layers). You cannot see any flaw in the Merciful (God's) creation. Look again, can you make out any rifts?"(Koran 67:3)

If we deny the Koran's claim of being God's revelation, we have to account for the above information, and how it made its way into the Koran, always without error, and always accurate. Justice and truth demand that or we are fooling ourselves alone.

Falsification Tests:

The Koran offers what is not offered by religions, generally speaking. It offers what the scientific community demands before they even listen to any new theory, *falsification tests*, based on Karl Popper's *Critical Rationalism*. The Koran presents itself with tests to disprove it, if it is false.

1. The Koran in 4:82 challenges people to find a mistake or contradiction in the book and hence disqualify it, if it is indeed a lie.

2. The Koran talks about people and how they will behave. If they were to act contrary to how the Koran pre-told their behavior, it would be disqualified.
   Muhammad had an uncle by the name of Abu-Lahab. This man hated Muhammad and was always strong in opposing him. Many years before the man died, the small chapter in the Koran documented his behavior, saying that he will be condemned and will never change (Koran 111:1-5). All he had to do to prove the Koran wrong was say: *"I am a Muslim, I change my behavior, your book is wrong."* Yet he never did do it, never thought of it even though he would have loved to.

3. The Koran claims that in a pluralistic society, the Christians would always treat the Muslims better than the Jews and Idolaters (Koran 5:85,86). Now scan the world scene where Jews, Christians and Muslims live together. Are the Jews closer to the Muslims or the Christians?
   The only thing the Jews have to do to disprove the Koran is to band together and treat the Muslims better than the Christians do for a little while and the Koran is disproved. Yet this has not happened and given the reputation of the Koran, never will.

4. The Koran says that if it is not what it claims to be then people should produce a document comparable to the Koran (2:23 etc). Comparison criteria would be what I have discussed earlier: i) It should contain information, which no one knows today, but will be found out tomorrow as scientifically accurate. ii) It should contain falsification tests as the Koran. iii) It should stand the test of "forgery" and "hallucination" as the Koran does. iv) It should give "sound" scientifically testable social advice as the Koran. v) Equal the Koran on literary merits. vi) Should have God speaking in the first person as the Koran does and then pass the test of inerrancy.
   In the face of all the facts that the Koran provides, it is evident that it challenges human intellect and explanation and presents itself as

a challenge to traditional religion and skeptical scientists. In the light of this, let us consider this statement that it makes:

If all of humankind and other intelligent species (Jinn) were to band together to produce the like of this Koran, they would not be able to, even if they backed up each other with help and support (Koran 17:89).

Bibliography:

1. Miller, Gary. *The Amazing Quran.* (Video Recording, transcribed, Sept 1990, by Muhammed A. Asadi. Lahore, Pakistan).

2. Asadi, Muhammed A. 1992. *Koran: A Scientific Analysis*. Lahore. Pakistan.

3. Asadi, Muhammed A. 1995. *The Message of Qur'an and Islam*. Lahore, Pakistan: Ferozsons' Ltd.

4. Asadi, Muhammed A. 2000. The Unifying Theory of Everything: Koran & Nature's Testimony. Writer's Club Press. New York.

5. Koran. Translated from the Arabic.

6. Bucaille, Maurice. *What is the Origin of Man?* 1987. Seghers, Paris.

7. Bucaille, Maurice. *The Bible, the Qur'an and Science*. 1985. Seghers. Paris.

8. Rehaili. Abdullah. M. *This is the Truth*. 1995. Riyadh. Saudi Arabia.

Other references used are narrated and acknowledged within the text, in full, for clarity.

Say: "O People of the Book! Come to conciliatory terms as between us and you: That we worship none but God; that we associate no partners with him; that we take not, from among ourselves, Lords and Keepers other than God."

If then they turn away, say: "Bear witness that we are Muslim (submitters to God)."

—(Koran 3:64)

0-595-21258-1

Printed in the United States
1160500002B/152